DEVELOPING A
SPIRITUAL
WARFARE
MENTALITY
—— in the ——
Midst of the Valley

DEVELOPING A
SPIRITUAL
WARFARE
MENTALITY
—— in the ——
Midst of the Valley

STANLEY R. SAUNDERS

Library of Congress Control Number: 2012902265
ISBN: Hardcover   978-1-4691-6369-7
                Softcover   978-1-4691-6368-0
                Ebook   978-1-4691-6370-3

This book was printed in the United States of America.

Editor: Ms. Gilda Tucker

E-mail address: *stanleysaunders@hotmail.com*

Stanley R. Saunders
P.O box #681
Belize City, Belize
Central America

To order additional copies of this book, contact:
Xlibris Corporation
1-888-795-4274
www.Xlibris.com
Orders@Xlibris.com
109709

CONTENTS

DEDICATION

It is with a sincere heart that I dedicate this book to the following persons:

Ms. Sandra McClaren, my mother—for your unwavering support and encouragement; you have been a true inspiration to my siblings and me. It is because of you that we have become productive and respectable citizens in our country, Belize.

Mr. and Mrs. Ensford Maskall—for your dedication in nurturing spiritual sons and daughters for the Kingdom of God; I have seen the fruits of your labour, so I want to say, thank you.

All the beautiful and wonderful people of Belize and the world, at large, I pray and hope that you will always make God your priority. This is the only way you will find the meaning and purpose in life. Stay in intimacy with the Lord, and live in accordance with the values of His kingdom.

ACKNOWLEDGMENTS

THERE IS A famous proverb that says, 'No man is an island.'
I extend appreciation and gratitude to the following persons who helped to make this book a reality:

Firstly, Ms. Sandra McClaren, my mother, who made me believe that I can do all things through Christ who strengthens me.

Mrs. Kimberly Martinez, a friend, whose timely advice, critiquing, and suggestions were priceless.

Ms. Gilda Tucker, my former teacher, who took time out of her busy schedule and edited this book.

Mr. Brian Plummer, a co-worker, whose critiquing and encouragement were vital during this long process.

Finally, Mr. Sylburn Arthurs, a dear friend and mentor, who encouraged and challenged me to complete this journey, and offered timely feedback.

INTRODUCTION

H AVE YOU EVER wondered why you experience so many ups and downs? Have you ever questioned the purpose of your trials and testing, especially when they do not seem to make sense? We all grapple with these questions as we journey through life. In spite of life's challenges and difficulties, remember that God always has our best interest at heart, and He continually works on our behalf. Isn't that amazing?

Nevertheless, most of us, no matter how mature we seem to be, wrestle with these truths from time to time. Sometimes when we go through different circumstances and struggles, we get so short-sighted and self-centered that we often lose sight of the bigger picture, as outlined in the book of Romans:

> And we know that in all things God works for the good of those who love him who have been called according to his purpose. (Rom. 8:28)

I want you to understand that from the moment you enter into a relationship with Christ, you have essentially put yourself in a position to be processed by God. This means you are a kingdom-product that God is perfecting every day. Everything that happens in your life is a clear indication that you are being transformed into the image of Christ. The character of Christ is invading and shaping your life.

I know it seems unfair that God often allows us to go through trials and tribulations to complete this 'perfection process', but I assure you that God has your best interest at heart, and He knows what He is doing.

God is very interested in you. In fact, all God thinks about is humanity—His treasured possession. God wants you to reach your greatest potential here on earth, but you cannot reach that level until you learn to think and function like God. The height of confronting spiritual warfare is to think and function like God in the realm of the earth.

It is important to understand that this is a lifelong process. Sometimes the world can feel like a lonely and frustrating place, but for us, there is a purpose. When we begin to think and function like God, our environment automatically begins to change and we experience very fruitful and productive lives. We also begin to look at things differently and pursue opportunities to reach out to a hurting humanity, searching for truth and light.

This book will not focus a great deal on magnifying or giving any unnecessary credit to Satan, our enemy. It is my belief that most believers focus too much on the attacks of the enemy and lose sight of God in the midst of their circumstances. In other words, they perceive everything that is happening to them as a negative attack from the devil; consequently, they spend a great deal of time rebuking devils and refusing to make changes in their own personal lives. This is not to say that evil does not exist or that there is no devil; but we need to learn to focus more on what God is establishing through us.

I believe that God is building a mature people. By this, I mean that He is raising up a generation of people with uncompromising mentalities and values, who will not be afraid to penetrate the systems of the earth with the truth of God's Word. Sometimes, as believers, we are afraid to represent and speak the truth because of the possible consequences. Maybe in doing so, we might lose friends and/or other relationships, people might dislike us, or we might even lose our jobs. In spite of that, I believe that God is calling His people to function beyond the fears of the world and simply live for Him. Regardless of the cost, we need to live for Him because it is only in Him that we can fulfill our God-ordained destiny:

'For [even the whole] creation (all nature) waits expectantly and longs earnestly for God's sons to be made known [waits for the revealing, the disclosing of their sonship].' (Rom. 8:19)

The above Scripture is very profound because it shows the current state of the earth. All of creation, especially mankind, is in a 'waiting state'. The word 'waits' in this context means 'to look for'. In other words, mankind is waiting for that day when they can see and experience the fullness of God through us, His children. There is a serious demand placed on the sons of God because we can no longer function from a place, where we just exist and live life as it comes. People want and need to experience hope in the midst of their hopeless situations. The world is crying out for us to step things up to another level. Can you sense the level of desperation that the earth is experiencing? What we are hearing on the news and seeing—before our very eyes—is a loud cry for the people of God to give biblical solutions to a hurting and dying world.

STANLEY R. SAUNDERS

Who are you? You are a representation of God on earth! What authority do you have? You have the authority and the resources of heaven to enable you on earth to become a distinct and impacting individual. Consequently, the impact that you have on this earth will be permanent, lasting for generations to come. The devil is afraid of you because of your spiritual bloodline. It's in your spiritual genes: You have the capacity to walk, think, talk, and function like Christ in the realms of the earth. Therefore, as you take up your spiritual mantle, the world cannot help but take notice and ask you, 'Who is your God? And why is it that you are continually experiencing success?' They will also say, 'How can I get that? I need what you have in my life!'

We are engaged in battle! Let us establish that the very gates of hell and every demon and dirty devil is afraid of whom you are in Christ. Once your true identity in Christ is discovered, you begin to function differently on this earth, and it is a clear signal that darkness no longer has a foothold in your life. It's freedom time! It's a joyous occasion! It is time to celebrate, for your victory is at hand. When you get to this point in your life, it simply means that you have developed a 'warfare mentality'. You have decided that you will no longer be consumed by life's circumstances, and you will stand in the midst of the valley. You are fully convinced that your breakthrough is at hand, and you want all that God has in store for you.

Friends, that is the place of triumph that Christ wants us to inhabit. It's our birthright! You were created to be prosperous and successful in life. God has called us 'overcomers'. This is more than a fact; it's a reality

> For I know the plans I have for you, declares the LORD, 'plans to prosper you and not to harm you, plans to give you hope and a future.' (Jer. 29:11, NIV)

Can you argue against the Word? God has made it plain in His Word that He has our best interest at heart. The *Message Bible* puts it this way:

> [11]'I'll show up and take care of you as I promised and bring you back home. I know what I'm doing. I have it all planned out—plans to take care of you, not abandon you, plans to give you the future you hope for.' (Jer. 29:11)

I can imagine that as God was creating you in the design room, He was declaring victory, hope, prosperity, joy, peace, sound mind, wealth, health, and salvation over your life. How profound is that? I want you to grab hold of that as God continues to speak to you, regardless of what stage you are in your walk with Him.

This book will help to equip you for the ongoing warfare of life. Your mind will be opened and transformed by the life-changing truth of God's Word. I want the best for you. Let's step up our kingdom-living to another dimension as together we experience all that God has in store for us. You are about to experience tremendous breakthroughs in your health, thoughts, finances, emotions, family, job, church community, business affairs, relationships, and every other aspect of your life. Are you ready?

CHAPTER 1

Understanding Spiritual Warfare: What is the Origin of this Concept?

B Y DEFINITION, A war is an active struggle between two entities or the waging of armed conflict against an enemy. Another definition of 'warfare' is 'a state of open, armed, often prolonged conflict carried on between nations, states or parties'. One person describes war as an attempt by one country (or side, in a civil war) to impose its will on another. The key element or objective that all wars have in common is the gaining of dominion, and history has repeatedly proven that men have always been in pursuit of territorial dominion. Many countries were birthed as a result of some significant war that occurred decades, centuries, or millenniums ago, which resulted in some sort of freedom, democracy, identity, or sovereignty from another country or territory.

A nation is very likely to engage in war or bolster its military defence system if she believes that her territorial domain is being threatened by any other country. In fact, according to an article written in *The Washington Post,* the wars in Iraq and Afghanistan have cost the United States of America approximately $720 million each day, which placed the total cost of the Iraq war at more than $2.2 trillion. Regardless of your view on this, it simply shows the extent to which a country would go to reinforce its dominion in the earth.

Moreover, world history has been defined by several significant wars, such as World War I, World War II, the United States of America Civil War, American Revolution, Vietnam War, Korean War, Iraq War, French Revolution, Persian Wars, and Punic Wars. This is very significant because it says a lot about the mentalities of human beings who have always been fighting for freedom, domination, and sovereignty. As human beings, we do not like to feel threatened and inferior. We somehow take pride in the sovereignty and the territorial dominion for which our forefathers have fought. Hence according to the historical accounts, it is safe to suggest that a warfare mentality is an inherent quality within each and every person, and its origin can be traced back to the book of Genesis. Let us carefully examine the Scripture below:

> Then God said, 'Let us make man in our image, according to our likeness; *let them have dominion* . . . over all the earth and over every creeping thing that creeps on the earth.' So God created man in His own image; in the image of God He created him; male and female He created them. Then God blessed them, and God said to them, ' . . . *Have dominion.*' (Gen. 1:26-27)

In Genesis, Chapter 1, a significant interaction that forever changed the course of history occurred between God and His creation. He (God) created man with the will, desires, thoughts, and the capacity to have dominion over all the earth *(Read Genesis, Chapter 1, carefully)*. In Hebrew, the word 'dominion' means 'to rule or reign', and it suggests to dominate or to exercise authority over. This concept actually came from God because He had the idea to establish His kingdom on earth through man. Mankind was given the authority, capacity, and charge to rule earth on God's behalf. Therefore, as God breathed life into Adam, the culture of a 'warfare mentality' and 'dominion' became entrenched deeply within his spirit—man. Adam was instantly created a warrior by spirit and soul because his creator (God) designed and engineered him that way so that he could rule the earth and set the precedence for generational warriors, born of his genes, who would exercise dominion as well. A warfare mentality is an ongoing process, whereby individuals are learning to think according to the values and culture of God's kingdom so they can function with accuracy, consistency, and relevance on the earth.

I can imagine God saying to him daily, 'Adam, have dominion over this territory (earth) for Me—rule it, exercise authority over it, steward it, defend it—don't allow anything that is not of Me to take root, and be a king in the earth.' That was Adam's primary responsibility! I often hear people debate the trust factor between Adam and God: Why did God trust Adam, especially when He knew what would happen? This is an interesting question, and I will answer it in this way. I believe that God trusted Adam because He trusted Himself. Remember, the Scripture says that man was created in the image and likeness of God. Therefore, when He looked at Adam, God saw Himself.

STANLEY R. SAUNDERS

Adam was a direct reflection of God, and God enjoyed looking at Himself. That phenomenon can be likened to a confident person who enjoys staring at him or her/self in the mirror. That's how God felt about Adam, His prized creation, and He could not help but trust him. Remember, God created Adam with strength, wisdom, talent, leadership, discernment, intelligence, free will, emotions, and every other attribute that He (God) has. This means the definition of 'Adam' is essentially 'God released or expressed' on the earth.

Furthermore, Adam naturally had the warfare mentality that has been passed down from generation to generation. All human beings possess this characteristic regardless of age, sex, race, social background, colour, genetics, status, education, and religion. In fact, I would go so far as to say that there is nothing that can take this mentality away from you; it is sealed deep within your soul and spirit. Have you ever wondered why you don't like to lose? Why do you get upset when things are out of order around you? Why do you, at times, feel like you are not from this earth? Why do you have a passion for investment? Why is it that you always want to change your environment and the people around you? Why is it that, deep within, you don't want to live in sin? It is simply the way God designed you!

There is nothing wrong with you! You were not created to live an insignificant life. It is within you to want to rule, dominate, lead, reign, and take authority. This is your true human nature because God designed you that way from before the very foundations of the earth! However, even though this quality cannot be taken away, it can be suppressed and/or perverted. In fact, this is what the Prince of Darkness does on a consistent basis so that this positive God-given quality is never developed, harnessed, and released in accordance with the principles of God's Word.

The devil wants to influence your mentality so that you may never accomplish the will of God for your life. The truth about dominion is that it starts in the mind and then it manifests into physical and practical actions. In regard to spiritual warfare, you need to understand that there are two different systems that are battling for the exclusive rights of your mind: the Kingdom of Darkness (the world or Babylon) and the Kingdom of God.

The Scripture says that as a man thinks in his heart so is he *(Pro. 23:7)*. The true battle is in the mind. If you get the mind, you get the heart. If you get the heart, you get the man's destiny. That is why mentality is so important to God. It is equally important to the devil. He is desperately fighting to affect our mentalities because this is where spiritual warfare starts. There is an ongoing wrestling match between your spirit and your flesh. But the good news is that you have the authority to dictate who wins this crucial match. *God has put you in charge of your destiny; you have the power to choose.* Why do you think that the devil attempts to bring seeds of discouragement, frustration, condemnation, depression, anxiety, fear, insecurity, sadness, and inferiority? All of these negative emotions are triggered in the mind. These are not from God. I want us to further examine Proverbs 23:7 to give you a more vivid explanation as to how powerful your mind is. Let's look at the Scripture again:

> Proverbs 23:7 (Amplified Bible) 7 For as he thinks in his heart, so is he. As one who reckons, he says to you, eat and drink, yet his heart is not with you [but is grudging the cost].

This passage of the Scripture is interesting because it puts the power of the mind in the driver's seat. The word 'thinks' in Hebrew is 'sha`ar', which means 'to split open, reason out, calculate, reckon, or estimate'. The expression 'split open' is not making reference to a literal translation or understanding. In the physical sense, when you split open something, you see value beyond the surface. In other words, you see the value of the substance inside. For example, a lot of people use the coconut for varied purposes: the liquid inside is used as a drink; the edible meat is used as food; it is also used fresh or dry in cooking and to make 'coconut oil' used for both cooking and making margarine. If you are not able to split the coconut open, you will never experience the hidden core and nutritional value that are beyond the surface of the hard shell.

Spiritually, the mind is so powerful that it is capable of seeing value beyond the hard surface and the circumstances of life. We need to renew our minds to begin to see things in the spiritual realm so that we can enhance the objective for God's kingdom. Spiritual warfare is about living beyond what your physical eyes perceive. Remember, you can only enjoy the coconut if you split it open. Therefore, in life, God is challenging us to look beyond the surface and experience the purpose and joys of life. Victory starts with your mentality!

Let's look at Proverbs 23:7 differently. As a man splits open and sets a price (mentally and spiritually) on something, he will think, desire, pursue, and subdue it. You are a victim of your mentality! A man will have what he sees. I like to look at it this way: Your mind has the power to reveal the limitless possibilities of the Kingdom of God. Therefore, you are responsible for the development of your mind. To what are you exposing your mind? Whatever you expose your mind to is what it will produce. For example, if you expose it to love, it will think and produce thoughts of love. If you expose it to fear and inferiority, then it will produce fruits of fear and inferiority. I believe that, more than anything, God is challenging us to maintain sound and healthy minds so that we can make accurate 'kingdom' decisions.

What Did Adam Fail to Understand?—The Power of Maintenance

Even though God commissioned Adam to have dominion in the earth, Adam did not understand the price and principles of dominion. We need to understand that in life everything has a **'purchase price'** as well as a maintenance price. Dominion is the by-product of what I described earlier as a warfare mentality. In simple terms, your mentality will determine what you will dominate. Therefore, in order to maintain dominion, you have to maintain a sound mentality, which is your key to fruitfulness in the realms of the earth. If a country wins a war and the government decides the next day to dissolve the army, what do you think will happen?

Even though the country is experiencing victory, if the enemy decides to strike back, then the other country will likely lose everything for which it had fought. In regard to Adam, God gave him everything that he needed in order to have dominion, and he did not maintain it. I believe he had a mental lapse, and the enemy was able to invade that area and cause havoc. I want you to always remember the principle that having dominion today does not guarantee dominion tomorrow. That is why every day, when we read God's Word, we must meditate on His principles and apply them so that we reinforce dominion in the realms of our world. If you get a brand new Mercedes Benz, and you do not maintain it, then eventually the vehicle will malfunction even though it has various potentials. Our minds function under those same principles. If we want our minds to function the way God originally designed them, then we constantly have to expose them to kingdom values. This is the only way we will get optimum productivity from our minds.

Be Careful! A Warfare Mentality Can be and has Been Perverted!

Our Heavenly Father is not a God that terrorises His children with threats that intimidate and cause them to panic. He wants the best for you! As human beings, we desperately need to possess strong minds. If you do not possess a strong mind, you will not experience any victory in spiritual warfare. This is the truth: God has naturally given us a spiritual warfare mentality to exercise His will (purpose) in the realms of the earth. There is a reason for your existence: to bring forth the purpose of God in your family, workplace, community, city, and nation. God's kingdom is actually expanding when you continue to influence the mentalities of the people around you, which, in turn, will eventually cause a transformation or a reshaping of your community.

If you do not 'take a stand', darkness will rule and conquer. God has given you a conquering mentality. However, if this quality is not channelled from the right heart, attitude, principles of government, then it will bear fruits of chaos and disaster on the earth. Surprise, surprise! What is happening on the earth right now? We are reaping disaster, chaos, perversion, corruption, violence, etc. The root of all these negative vibes is a messed up mentality!

The fall of man is one of the most talked about and debated Bible concepts today. The truth behind it is that when Adam sinned against God by his selfishly disobedient act, he essentially broke fellowship and intimacy with God *(Read Gennesis Chapter 2)*. In addition, the DNA of sin (a scarred mentality) entered and scarred humanity from that point onward. Man lost his righteousness status and began to think and function from a place of blindness, ignorance, and selfishness. Let's read *Romans 5:12-14:*

> You know the story of how Adam landed us in the dilemma we're in—first sin, then death, and no one is exempt from either sin or death. That sin disturbed relations with God in everything and everyone, but the extent of the disturbance was not clear until God spelled it out in detail to Moses. So death, this huge abyss separating us from God, dominated the landscape from Adam to Moses. Even those who didn't sin precisely as Adam did by disobeying a specific command of God still had to experience this termination of life, this separation from God. But Adam, who got us into this, also points ahead to the One who will get us out of it. (The Message)

STANLEY R. SAUNDERS

When man sinned and began to think and function from a place of selfishness, the world became increasingly wicked and violent. The Scripture states:

> [5]The LORD saw how great man's wickedness on the Earth had become, and that every inclination of the thoughts of his heart was only evil all the time. [6]The LORD was grieved that he had made man on the Earth, and his heart was filled with pain. (Gen. 6:5) NIV

In other words, there was an increase in idolatry, murder, rape, incest, violence, robbery, theft; you name it, it was there on the earth and displeased a Holy God. He (God) also mentioned how sorry He was for creating man, whose heart was so wicked. In fact, it got so bad that God had to destroy the earth by water and wipe out so many generations of people who had a corrupt warfare mentality.

What's the Point?

The point behind all this is that sin actually perverts the true essence of a warfare mentality. Sin is a warfare mentality channelled and fuelled by a negative and selfish attitude. That is how the devil and his cohorts function. Even though Adam was the first man to sin, sin existed long before Adam. Let's look at the father of sin in Revelation 12:7-9:

> [7-12]War broke out in Heaven. Michael and his Angels fought the Dragon. The Dragon and his Angels fought back, but were no match for Michael. They were cleared out of Heaven, not a sign of them left. The great Dragon—ancient Serpent, the one called Devil and Satan, the one who led the whole earth astray—thrown out, and all his Angels thrown out with him, thrown down to Earth.

The devil, Satan, the enemy, the Prince of Darkness, Abaddon, Accuser of the Brethren, Adversary (one who stands against), Angel of the Bottomless Pit, Angel of Light, Dragon, is the father (origin) of sin. He is a former CEO of Worship, living in disgrace with an agenda to kill, steal, and destroy the people on the earth. Therefore, he sought out to destroy Adam with the luscious delicacies of sin. But before sin was manifested through the actual eating of the fruit, darkness essentially entered humanity when man purposed in his heart to believe the lies of the enemy. Consequently, Adam lost conception of the original purpose of spiritual warfare because he believed the thoughts and philosophy of the enemy and acted upon those beliefs.

Adam lost his sense of purpose on earth and relinquished the keys of the kingdom and dominion to the powers of darkness. Imagine this! Adam had the God-given capacity to discern the devil, and the God-given authority to cast the devil out of the garden because Adam was like God. He should have dealt with the devil with record quickness since he had been delegated and anointed to function as God on the earth. He messed up badly. The free will that God had given him was so powerful that he could have chosen to function like God in one moment, and, in another moment, he could have functioned like a cowardly wimp, as though he had no authority, power, and responsibility. I guess the devil caught him napping on one of those days and sin entered the human bloodline from that point onwards.

When you are separated from God, you no longer think and function like God. In fact, you function like and become a victim of the world; your way of doing things is contrary to the Word and will of God. For example, you might become gravitated towards lustful desires such as pornography, adultery, fornication, anger, bitterness, covetousness, or even murder. The world's way of doing things cannot please God because His laws are supreme and light and darkness cannot coexist. Please note that God will never compromise His laws to please anybody; He is a Holy God and, as His people, we must respond to Him in a holy manner if we are to please Him.

The Jesus Factor!

Thank you, Lord! Even though our granddaddy messed up, God was ready to deal with sin and reconcile man unto Himself for eternity. His plan was one that included a great sacrifice. In fact, in order to redeem mankind, God had to sacrifice the most precious thing that He had—Jesus, His son. He did not hesitate and willingly offered that sacrifice. Now, because of that blood-covenant sacrifice, we are free from the burden of sin, and we can once again be reconciled to God and think and function as He does in the earth. What happened at Calvary returned man the access to the mind of Christ:

STANLEY R. SAUNDERS

[16]For who has known or understood the mind (the counsels and purposes) of the Lord so as to guide and instruct Him and give Him knowledge? *But we have the mind of Christ (the Messiah) and do hold the thoughts (feelings and purposes) of His heart.* (1 Cor. 2:16; Amplified Bible)

We have access to the mind of Christ! On the same note, spiritual warfare is about cultivating this mentality in the earth so that changes occur on a personal, family, professional, corporate, communal, and national level. However, it is very important to note that changes start at an individual level; therefore, the more we change internally by upgrading our mentalities to the doctrine of the kingdom, the more our surroundings will be transformed. Why? Because we need to grasp, at a deeper level, that we are God's authorised change agents in the earth.

We have been summoned by God to facilitate His reign in every sector of society, especially where He plants us. Whether you are a doctor, musician, lawyer, politician, engineer, teacher, politician, or whatever your field is, God wants you to reflect kingdom values so that your light may shine. You are not a mere man; don't ever believe that satanic lie. Hence it is important to have the right attitude and perception of yourself and surrounding. That is why Paul said:

[1]IF THEN you have been raised with Christ [to a new life, thus sharing His resurrection from the dead], aim at and seek the [rich, eternal treasures] that are above, where Christ is, seated at the right hand of God. [2]*And set your minds and keep them set on what is above (the higher things), not on the things that are on the earth.* (Col. 2:1-2; Amplified Bible)

Paul is instructing the people of God to change their way of thinking. We ought not to think as the world thinks because we will simply reap corruption and disaster. So then, the challenge is to tune your mind to the frequency of God's Word, which will bring you to a great sense and place of purpose. This requires discipline and perseverance; nevertheless, it is possible for you to unveil the character of God in any given situation, regardless of the circumstances.

You have access to the mind of Christ; this is a statement, which you should never take lightly. God can be accessed by man; however, man also has the power and the will to deny that access. As human beings, we can choose to consult either God or some other source. But the problem with the latter is that we will reap undesirable consequences. Society has been paying the consequences of bad decisions men have made without applying Godly wisdom.

Moreover, the heart of spiritual warfare is not about changing the devil or chasing the devil. We need to be reminded constantly of the objective of this concept, which is capturing the right thoughts, attitude, mood, imagination, vision, and heart of God and invading the earth, our world, with an agenda to further His will (purpose). This is not a religious concept; it is a culture that God is creating on the earth through the hearts of His people.

When we achieve this, we will begin to penetrate the hearts of people who are crying out for significance and peace in their lives. They will observe us and realise that there is something different about us by the way we carry ourselves. Indeed, deep down, they will be searching for what we have and represent (abundant spiritual life). Don't miss the opportunity to let us penetrate the earth with the essence of God, through our lifestyle.

CHAPTER 2

A Tale of Two Distinctive Valleys

SPIRITUAL WARFARE IS one of the most misunderstood concepts in the Bible. Most believers do not understand the true concept and purpose of spiritual warfare. There are many believers who go around hunting for and chasing devils out of every situation and people they encounter. I am not saying that, at times, there is not the need for exorcism, but we have to be very discerning in every situation that life presents. The concept of spiritual warfare is way beyond the casting out of devils and demons.

It is about capturing and establishing the right mentality in every given situation that life presents so that you can function accurately in your God-ordained purpose. If you are able to capture the right mentality in any given situation, then you have to put yourself in a position of victory. Why? The right mentality represents the right heart, which is the primary concern of God. I believe that the more you allow the Word of God to affect your mentality, then the more God can elevate and use you. As believers, we need to understand that God is pleased when we reflect the values of the Kingdom of God in our families, work place, community, and in everything we do or in which we are involved. Let us examine 2 Corinthians 10:3-6 (The Message)

> 3-6The world is unprincipled. It's dog-eat-dog out there! The world doesn't fight fair. But we don't live or fight our battles that way—never have and never will. The tools of our trade aren't for marketing or manipulation, but they are for demolishing that entire massively corrupt culture. We use our powerful God-tools for smashing warped philosophies, tearing down barriers erected against the truth of God, fitting every loose thought and emotion and impulse into the structure of life shaped by Christ. Our tools are ready at hand for clearing the ground of every obstruction and building lives of obedience into maturity.

One of the key points that Paul made in the passage of the Scripture is that the culture of the Kingdom of God is different from that of the world. A man's culture determines how he will think, talk, sing, recreate, eat, worship, walk, socialise, work, and fight (war). The world (the system of darkness) will do things its way because it has been seasoned and conditioned to do so.

This is why we should not be frightened and surprised by the behaviours of people around us. I notice that people who are wicked are never shy about their wicked behaviours. They are good at being wicked because that is who they are, and they seem to have no choice but to express that nature. It's all cultural for them! Similarly, as representatives and agents of the Kingdom of God, we should never be afraid to express our culture by the way we think, talk, behave, and function. This is a challenge from God.

The name of this book is *Developing a Spiritual Warfare Mentality in the Midst of the Valley*. There is something powerful about a valley that defines the purpose of humanity. Regardless of where you are in your life, God uses valleys to fashion your mentality. Consequently, depending on how you respond to these two distinctive valleys will determine the level of breakthrough that you will experience in your life. Let's explore these two concepts so that we do not fall into the trap of negative thinking.

What is the Valley?

In the geographical context, a 'valley' is 'a long low area of land, often with a river or stream running through it, surrounded by higher ground. It's a depressed area that is often bounded by a river or hill' (Encarta Dictionary). If you want to find a valley, someone will usually instruct you to go to the southernmost part of an area. In the context of life, most people view a valley as a low mental state, usually characterised by frustration, anger, fear, anxiety, regret, pain, condemnation, depression, and discontent caused by either foreseen or unforeseen events.

It is a period during which you begin to question God. You begin to seek answers to your perceived problems. You also begin to question when your 'breakthrough' is coming as you wait impatiently and expectantly for God to move on your behalf. During this period, you begin to evaluate your life, and sometimes waiting for one day could seem like an eternity, especially if you feel like you did not deserve what is happening to you.

You begin to question: Why has this happened to me? What did I do wrong? Why are my neighbours so prosperous and they are not serving God?

Why me? Why is God allowing the wicked to prevail? If you made some bad decisions in your life, condemnation usually comes knocking at your door as guilt invites himself inside your heart. When you are at this place, sometimes you feel like God is far away from you, and He is nowhere to be found. To assist in achieving the objective of this book, I want to explain life to you, using two different analogies: the Valley of Bad Choices and the Valley of Destiny.

The Valley of Bad Choices: My 'Bad', God!

The valley of bad choices is no stranger to humanity. I want you to understand that many times, tribulations, hardships, and troubles occur in our lives as a result of wrong and poor choices that we make. It is very important for us to be reminded that Christians or believers are not exempted from the law of sowing and reaping, which is a universal law that applies to all of mankind. If you make bad choices in life, you will inevitably reap the consequences of that. In life, everything simply hinges on the decisions or choices that we make.

As human beings, we have been privileged to have the gift of freewill, meaning that we are free to choose. We can choose to act righteously or unrighteously in any given situation. However, it is important to note that our behaviours have consequences. If you chose to act righteously (obeying the principles of God's Word), then you will experience the unlimited and over-exceeding blessings, favour, and grace of God in every area of your life. On the contrary, if you chose to act unrighteously (disobeying the principles of God's Word), then you will reap corruption, sin, broken fellowship with God, and a curse. The Scripture says:

> 19-20I call Heaven and Earth to witness against you today: I place before you Life and Death, Blessing and Curse. Choose life so that you and your children will live. And love GOD, your God, listening obediently to him, firmly embracing him. Oh yes, he is life itself, a long life settled on the soil that GOD, your God, promised to give your ancestors, Abraham, Isaac, and Jacob. (Deut. 30:19; The Message)

The number of choices that we have to make on a daily basis, is amazing. God says that you can choose to obey, yet He pleads with man to obey; God is appealing to mankind to make right choices. Remember that God is deeply concerned about our overall well-being, but the very acts of disobedience push us further away from Him into a desolate land of hopelessness and curse, which is not God's original intent for our lives.

For example, I know of a person who got into serious debt as a result of poor spending habits and lack of prioritising. He spent his income foolishly without any regard for saving and proper investments. He even stopped tithing. Surprisingly, he ended up being upset with God to the point where he almost stopped serving Him because of the difficulties that he was experiencing in his life. Remember, this came as a result of his poor spending habits. The Bible cautions us to be good stewards of the things that God has entrusted to us:

> For it will be like a man going on a journey, who called his servants and entrusted to them his property. To one he gave five talents, to another two, to another one, to each according to his ability. Then he went away. He who had received the five talents went at once and traded with them, and he made five talents more. So also he who had the two talents made two talents more. But he who had received the one talent went and dug in the ground and hid his master's money . . . (Matt. 25:14-30)

The man with only one talent did not make a proper investment; therefore, he reaped nothing because he had sown nothing. You will always reap what you sow in life. As human beings, we always have to be very careful of the decisions that we are making because it is only a matter of time before we will reap what was sown. What have you been sowing? What have you been reaping? Maybe you are a young man or young lady who got caught up in a serious 'unequally yoked' relationship that you knew was not God's will for your life, yet you persisted; consequently, it has caused you pain, bitterness, hurt, and frustration. In the Bible, 2 Corinthians 6:14 says:

> Be ye not unequally yoked together with unbelievers: for what fellowship hath righteousness with unrighteousness? And what communion hath light with darkness? (KJV)

Today, many people are being diagnosed with all types of sicknesses and diseases that came as a result of poor eating habits. They did not take care of the temple of the Holy Spirit! I am not saying all this to condemn anyone because there is no condemnation for those who are in Christ Jesus. What I want is for you to understand that the valley of bad decision is real, and my reminding that you will reap bad fruits should not be regarded as a cliche. In other words, you should never take the reality of this valley lightly. A lot of people are reaping worthless harvests from bad seeds that they planted days, weeks, months, years, or decades ago.

Furthermore, the valley of bad decision is so powerful that it can also affect other people who have no influence on the decision that another has made. For example, a father's decision to spend his entire pay cheque on alcohol and drugs may affect the wife and children even though the father acted independently and selfishly. That is why we need to be very careful of the decisions that we make in life because they will affect us, but they can affect others as well. It saddens my heart whenever innocent people get hurt, especially when it comes as a result of somebody's poor judgement. Let us be reminded that it was the same thing that happened with Adam.

His decision still has a serious impact on humanity; that is why many people are struggling with sin. To be frank, I believe that, as God's people, we desperately need to be delivered from the vicious cycle of doing the same things but expecting different or pleasing results. Some people call this insanity. The law of sowing and reaping is universal. If you sow bad decisions, you will reap a harvest of bad consequences and a flawed lifestyle, which is not God's will for your life.

There is Good News for You!

I have some good news for you! You can choose to come out of this valley by first identifying your error, taking ownership of it, and then turning away. The word 'repent' simply means to think differently. What is amazing about God is that He knows your intents long before you even thought about them. We cannot fool God. Therefore, I am challenging you to a new level of humility in your life. You will not experience the abundance of God's favour, mercy, breakthrough, and grace unless you first identify destructive patterns of irrational thinking and decision-making and consciously turn away from them. That is true repentance!

As leaders, pastors, husbands, wives, singles, politicians, professionals, mothers, fathers, brothers, students, sisters, teachers, we have been making some costly decisions and God is now calling us from out of that place of darkness into His marvelous light. He is longing to have fellowship with us. He wants to dialogue with His chosen people, but disobedience (sin) hinders that process. God hates the fact that sometimes our actions create a barrier between mankind and Him. He is constantly thinking about His people. I find it amazing that we are always on His mind. I once heard somebody say that God thinks about nothing but human beings. That is really an accurate and profound statement. Remember that before Adam sinned, God came up with an excellent plan to restore humanity because He loves us so much. He sacrificed His only begotten son so that we can have eternal access to His kingdom.

Furthermore, He (God) desperately wants to take you to a new level in your life. Are you ready to take ownership of your past mistakes and move on? Let's be delivered from past disobedience and ignorance and never, ever, go back to them. Now, you are at the place of repentance and humility, where God will begin to help you through your situation:

> The LORD is nigh unto them that are of a broken heart; and saveth such as be of a contrite spirit. (Ps. 34:18)

> For thus says the high and exalted One who lives forever, whose name is Holy, 'I dwell on a high and holy place, And also with the contrite and lowly of spirit In order to revive the spirit of the lowly and to revive the heart of the contrite.' (Isa. 57:17)

> He heals the brokenhearted and binds up their wounds. (Ps. 147:3)

Based upon the Scriptures, you see that God wants to redeem you from your past mistakes and failures if you are sincere and willing. This is the place where God begins to pick you up and restore you in accordance with the condition of your heart and His will. Remember all God wants to do here is to lead you on the right path of accurate thinking and decision-making only if you are willing to submit to Him. He is not a God that would manipulate you, so just yield your soul to the hands of the potter, knowing that He has your best interest at heart. Isn't God awesome?

A Simple Prayer (for the Valley of Bad Decision)

Father, I realise that I have been making some bad decisions, such as _____ in my life. Forgive me, O Lord, for causing You hurt through my disobedient actions. I turn my mind and my heart to You, O God. Open my eyes, Oh Lord, that I may walk in wisdom. I want to follow You. I want to know You. Reveal your heart to me so that I may live a purposeful life. In the name of Jesus, break every mentality and bondage that has been holding me back. I release myself to You. Have your way in my life I ask, with thanksgiving, in Jesus's name. *Amen!*

The Valley of Destiny

Unlike the valley of bad choices, the valley of destiny is very different in that it has nothing to do with the consequences of bad decision-making. There are things in life that just happen; we have no control over them, and we must be able to discern this so that we don't blame God or blame ourselves and live in serious condemnation. It is very unhealthy for you to blame yourself for those things over which you have absolutely no control. You need to become fully aware of this right now. When you understand this absolute, you learn how to approach difficult situations with a different mind-set.

[21]They preached the good news in that city and won a large number of disciples. Then they returned to Lystra, Iconium and Antioch, [22]strengthening the disciples and encouraging them to remain true to the faith. *'We must go through many hardships to enter the kingdom of God.'* (Acts 14:21)

Let us consider the life of Job:

[1]In the land of Uz, there lived a man whose name was Job. This man was blameless and upright; he feared God and shunned evil. [2]He had seven sons and three daughters, [3]and he owned seven thousand sheep, three thousand camels, five hundred yoke of oxen and five hundred donkeys, and had a large number of servants. He was the greatest man among all the people of the East. (Job 1:1-3)

As you have realised, everything was going so smoothly that even the devil took notice of how prosperous he was and declared him untouchable. Can you believe that? The enemy saw that the favour of the Lord was upon him in such abundance:

Satan replied. [10]'Have you not put a hedge around him and his household and everything he has? You have blessed the work of his hands, so that his flocks and herds are spread throughout the land.' (Job 1:10)

It is interesting to note that at this point in Job's life, he probably didn't expect the series of events that were about to unfold since he was journeying with God in perfect obedience. This is what happened to him:

1. All of his oxen and donkeys were gone.
2. He lost most of his servants.
3. His sheep were burnt.
4. His camels were raided.
5. He lost his children.
6. He was afflicted with pain and sickness.
7. He was depressed.
8. He was pressured by his wife to curse God and die.

Certainly, what happened to Job landed him in the 'Valley of Destiny'. Had he done anything wrong? Had he sinned against God? Was he in rebellion? No! Job's life demonstrates a classic example of the valley of destiny.

To be completely honest, most people want to hear a great sermon saying that God will bless them tremendously and they will never experience lack a day in their lives or that God will open up the windows of heaven and they will have blessings beyond what they can contain. Biblically speaking, God wants to bless His people, and I will not argue against the Word of God. But what I want you to grasp fully is that you will experience several valleys of destiny in your life, and you must be prepared to not only face but also overcome them, knowing that all things work together for good for those who love God:

[12]Dear friends, do not be surprised at the painful trial you are suffering, as though something strange was happening to you. [13]But rejoice that you participate in the sufferings of Christ, so that you may be overjoyed when his glory is revealed. (1 Pet. 4:12-13)

The valley of destiny will inevitably come your way! Therefore, it is your response to the valleys of life that will ultimately determine the level of blessings and breakthroughs that you will experience. *You do not determine whether it rains or not, but it is surely wise to get an umbrella.* As people of God, oftentimes we suffer from poor application of principles. I like to call this ignorance. Let's consider the life of Joseph. He was an upright young man before God and had not done anything to deserve what he went through: He experienced the bitter valley of life. However, praise be to God, he ultimately experienced great victory in his life!

People say that Joseph should not have told his brothers about his dreams. It is very important for us to be careful about whom we share our dreams and visions with because a lot of people tend to be negative about other people's dreams. However, Joseph's experiences with trials and tribulations had nothing to with the fact that he had spoken with his brothers. Joseph's life was 100 percent of God in full operation. Everything he went through was destiny, for God was in full control from the beginning to the end.

It is my firm belief that while Joseph was in slavery, he questioned God many nights. He must have said to himself: Why me, God? What did I do wrong? Where are the blessings of Abraham? He was probably upset with God many nights. This was a very difficult time in the life of Joseph, and I am certain that if God had told him in advance what he would be going through, he would have fled from his destiny. As human beings, we prefer to be comfortable. That is why whenever we face discomfort, we almost automatically begin to question God and put up some sort of mental and emotional resistance.

The Joseph Factor!

In spite of what Joseph was going through, there was something that propelled him forward in the midst of the trials and tribulations. He had to develop a superior mentality that enabled him to overcome his circumstances and establish the purposes of God. Maybe you have been facing some trials and tribulations that were not brought about by your actions. Maybe you are being persecuted for having integrity. You might not understand the reason. But I dare you to trust God in spite of what you are going through. It is not the end of the world. God will make a way where there seems to be no way. I am declaring that, as Joseph, you will overcome your circumstances.

Some Words of Wisdom

If you are facing a difficult time right now, don't get upset with God! I assure you that as you continue to trust in God, He will make things clear to you and reveal His purpose. Don't allow your circumstances to dictate how you respond to God. Be very careful that whom or/and what you are listening to do not mislead you. Like Joseph, push yourself forward and lift your head high. God has already made an escape plan for you. Things will not remain as they are—things will get better for you. Continue the good work! Don't give up on yourself and be encouraged because God never disappoints.

I have found God to be faithful and strong. Trust Him! He will make a way for you, especially when there seems to be no way. I challenge you to open your eyes. That was what Joseph had to do. He was far away from his comfort zone and was experiencing great rejection. Joseph probably felt he had the right to blame God because he had not done anything wrong. Nevertheless, he did not spend his life wallowing in pity; he persevered, serving Pharaoh with all diligence to the best of his ability, and God exalted him—he was rewarded.

Dealing with Pharaohs

Maybe you are working for a boss who is very demanding and overbearing, but I challenge you to keep serving diligently. Why? God always exalts the humble and the hardworking:

> [6]Humble yourselves, therefore, under God's mighty hand, that He may lift you up in *due time*. (1 Pet. 5:8)

The prerequisite for any promotion is humility. The Scripture teaches us that everybody has a due time. Therefore, you have the assurance that your due season is coming. Isn't that spiritually uplifting? So continue to persevere in humility, and, just as it was for Joseph, you will see the salvation of the Lord.

Maybe you are facing a difficult time in your life and you are not sure exactly what to do. I wish to point out that when you are not sure what to do, you are at a good place. Why? Because you now find yourself at a place where you can begin to consult God and respond based on His purpose for your life. When you consult God through prayer and earnest desire for Godly counsel, He releases a dimension of wisdom that will cause a tremendous change in your life. God wants you to consult Him and He desperately wants to make the crooked paths straight. God is never confused; therefore, He is ready to bring order and clarity in your life. Will you allow Him? Are you ready to go from the valley of bad decision to the valley of destiny?

A Simple Prayer (for the Valley of Destiny)

Father God, I really don't understand what is happening in my life. Open my eyes so that I may see what is happening. Help me not to get angry, for I know that You are doing a new thing in my life. Teach me how to trust in You, especially in difficult times. Like Joseph, I will persevere and push forward because I know that joy comes in the morning. I receive your peace in the midst of this storm. I declare that You are faithful, O God. I declare your sovereignty in the midst of my situation. Thank You that You have already made a way for me. I trust You, O Lord, and I put this situation under your control, in Jesus's name. *Amen*

CHAPTER 3

Understanding Opposition

WHENEVER YOU ARE trying to go forward, opposition will always come because every system of the world opposes the will of God. Remember that you carry the will of God in your heart. The amazing thing about life is that if you learn to respond to opposition in the right way, you will experience tremendous victories in everything that you do. Remember, you were created to experience victory in every area of your life. You were created to bear fruits in and out of season. That is what God desired when He created you.

I often listen to people saying they are going through this and that, and they can't minister because they are in pain. Did you know that that's not scriptural? That's nonsense! God has put you in a constant position to minister and to have victory. Joseph was ministering to people when he was in prison, and even when Jesus was on His road to a death sentence, He healed a man's ears. What is your excuse again?

As people of God, we need to rid ourselves of some mindsets such as, 'Oh, the Lord is resting me for a season. I am in a season of transition and therefore I cannot assist anyone.' That is a weak mentality. We are always transitioning from glory to glory in the Kingdom of God. There is a progressive and violent advancement in the Kingdom of God. As you grow spiritually, it expands because there is a direct relationship between your personal growth and its expansion. Jesus said that the Kingdom of God is within you (Luke 17:21). Of course, there are times for resting, but we don't have to live in a place of isolation, pity, and dormancy.

The mentality should always be *'God I am ready to advance'* or *'What's next, Lord?'* We should always be crying out: 'God, change my heart. I need you.' As I said earlier, God is building a strong-minded people, but everything starts and finishes with the right mentality of the people. If you search the Scriptures carefully, you will discover that whenever God wanted to do something on the earth, He had to seek out a man or woman with a forceful mentality. God knew that in order for man to execute His will in the earth, man had to rise above the mentality perpetuated by the kingdom of darkness, by modifying his thinking pattern and embracing that of his creator.

Defining Opposition

Let me give you a definition for the term 'opposition'. I believe that there are some ancient mentalities that we desperately need to demolish if we desire to go forward in Christ. God is calling us to renew our minds so that we can think and function like Christ in the realms of this earth. Opposition is any mind-set that conflicts or exalts itself above the will of God. What we need to understand is that mindsets will either bring forth or make stagnant the will of God. Therefore, the mentality of a people is very critical for any kind of kingdom advancement in the earth. Let's go to 2 Corinthians 10:3-6:

> [3]though we live in the world, we do not wage war as the world does. [4]The weapons we fight with are not the weapons of the world. On the contrary, they have divine power to demolish strongholds. [5]We demolish arguments and every pretension that sets itself up against the knowledge of God and we take captive every thought to make it obedient to Christ. [6]And we will be ready to punish every act of disobedience, once your obedience is complete. (NIV)

The key thing to take note of is that the source of opposition is within a negative mind-set that seeks to exalt itself and rise above the will of God. In other words, it is any mentality that is contrary to the Word of God. It is anti-kingdom because the Word of God does not support the very nature of negative thinking. I want to explain two types of oppositions: *Internal Opposition and External Opposition.*

External Opposition

By definition, external opposition is any force, situation, or climate influenced by a negative mind-set. Notice that I did not shorten the definition on purpose because the challenges that we are facing, in every aspect of our lives, are beyond people. In other words, your problem is not people. It is the mentality that is influencing the people. We tend to spend a great deal of time fighting people as though we are in a physical battle, and we constantly wear out ourselves, worrying about people and holding unnecessary offenses.

At the end of the day, you need to understand that the issue is not your boss. I know sometimes bosses can get on our nerves, right? The problem is not your gossiping co-worker; it's not your cheating, unfaithful husband or your outrageously rebellious offspring. Therefore, you need to change your fighting strategies and your perception of people in a given situation. By this, I mean that since it is a spiritual battle, you need to take a spiritual and practical approach to address the situation because it is important to understand that a physical, emotional, or even verbal showdown will eventually worsen the situation and ultimately lead to your demise physically, professionally, spiritually, mentally, or emotionally.

The second challenge is to change the way you view people because when you understand that it is not about people, then it is easy to show Godly love towards them, with no malice or ill intent. As kingdom citizens, we should not hate people but rather wage war against deceptive principalities (mentalities) that seek to destroy people. I have really been asking God to help me in this area of my life because sometimes it is difficult to see beyond the surface of men. Let's be real! Sometimes you want to literally beat some people and/or 'bless' them with some 'nice' curse words, right?

There were times when I would really 'get into it' with people, especially if they were what I describe as 'repeat offenders'. Thankfully, God has helped me to choose my battles carefully and to be very discerning in different situations. This is a serious place of maturity to which God is calling each of us. It is not a place for an overnight fix; it is for an absolute heart-surrender to God. Believe it or not, God measures your level of maturity by how much you love people, especially when they seem to come across as your enemies.

Internal Opposition

Now, let me introduce you to the most powerful type of opposition, which is called internal opposition. This type of opposition is more powerful because while you cannot directly control what is happening around you, you can surely control what is happening within you. Therefore, internal opposition is the source and nature of your response to the external oppositions. For example, if your co-worker, classmate, spouse, or neighbour curses you, you have a choice as to how you would respond to that person; you have full control over the way to respond. The burden is neither on the devil nor God. After all, you have been given a free will to make whatever decision you want to make. Would you indeed turn the other cheek?

I remember once during my boyhood, a reverend was teaching me, from the Scriptures, about turning the other cheek. I told her that as I turned one cheek, I was slapped on the other cheek (both cheeks got slapped), and so I had run out of cheeks. The reverend was teaching me a very important principle that I did not want to receive at that time. The principle that she was teaching me was simply this: *you need to learn how to respond to adversity.* I believe this is what God is teaching His people: you need to learn how to respond to difficulties. If you are able to master and develop this concept, then you will experience tremendous victory in every area of your life. This is a process in which you constantly have to engage yourself. I believe that we need to learn this concept (responding to adversity) at an individual and corporate level. This is the most important skill that you can ever develop in your life.

What is the Purpose of Opposition?

Why on earth does God allow certain things to happen? Have you ever posed such a question? What's up, God? One of the main reasons is that God allows opposition in order to show you the current condition of your heart. As a kingdom-person, you will constantly be tested by God. He wants to see your reaction because that determines your inner reality. He wants to unmask who you really are so that He can start His rebuilding project. Let's look at Ezekiel 36:26

> I will give you a new heart and put a new spirit in you; I will remove
> from you your heart of stone and give you a heart of flesh. (NIV)

In this passage of Scripture, God prophetically stated that He wants to subtract the stony heart. Why? A stony heart is the part of you that is cold towards God and others. It is the infected part of you that God wants to remove because it is selfish, egotistic, and independent of God. This is the area of your life that fights strongly to satisfy the flesh (self). Furthermore, the stony heart is unyielding and seeks to push you further away from the will of God; therefore, He allows adversity to come so that He can show you the current condition of your heart in an effort to help you deal with such and make major practical adjustments that serve His will.

It does not matter how anointed you think you are, or how long you have been attending church. You need to allow God to deal with your heart! The most dangerous feature of the stony heart is that it is anti-kingdom, meaning that it opposes the very advancement of the Kingdom of God. For example, if you are having difficulties in the workplace, then the stony heart would say, 'I will get out of the workplace because there are a lot of wicked people who are against me.'

Here is a question for you to ponder: *Are you praying for people to be saved or are you praying to be saved from people?* This is a very important question because again it challenges your heart. I am telling you God has been dealing with me in some of these areas. It is one thing to quote the Scriptures and memorise verses, but applying the Word of God in practical, real-life scenarios is a totally different ball game.

My Personal Story

When I first got into the teaching profession and when I realised how challenging it could be, I wanted to quit. I literally spent hours praying—and I think I even fasted—to get out. God showed me that it was not my environment that needed to be changed; it was my heart that needed immediate surgery. When God showed me that, I became very angry and upset. Why? I did not want to receive that word from Him.

To be very honest with you, I wanted God to respond to my prayer by giving me a new job. Therefore, I battled with that 'rhema' word for weeks because I wanted things to go my way and no other way. One day, I had a dreamlike experience in which God showed me a picture of a multitude of young people dying, and that was frightening to me. After a while, I humbled myself and began to make certain adjustments. Those specific adjustments started with a self-evaluation of my actions in relation to my purpose and role in the earth. Is it really God's will for me to just walk away from that environment? Who will help the young people? Who will disciple/mentor them? Those questions really flooded my mind after that eye-opening dream.

For me, it was a reality check, reminding me that I am here for a specific purpose; hence I must accomplish that purpose. That was a great cause

STANLEY R. SAUNDERS

for a mental adjustment. As I made those mental adjustments, I began to experience the grace of God in a way, which I had never expected, and I was much more functional in my workplace by relating to the young people differently. God has really put love in my heart for them. In addition to that, my prayer changed to 'Lord, use me as You will.' That has completely changed my life to date because I no longer see people as a problem, and I seek every opportunity to expand the Kingdom of God through my interaction with others. One of the hardest things for us to acknowledge is that we are the problem because most people, especially the Christians, don't like to be wrong. We like to blame other people for our problems, and, if we can't blame people, we blame the devil.

God is no respecter of persons; He just wants you to get it right. This has nothing to do with your educational status, economic status, or social background; this is all about God preparing you for greater kingdom work. I often hear people say God takes us to another level, and the more you surrender your heart, the more He can use you. Remember, the level at which God can use you is dependent on the quality and the condition of your heart. Let us further examine this concept.

A Closer Look at the Heart

According to the Merriam-Webster's Dictionary, the physical heart is 'a hollow muscular organ of vertebrate animals that by its rhythmic contraction acts as a force pump maintaining the circulation of the blood'. In other words, the heart is the organ that supplies blood and oxygen to all parts of the body. Its main purpose is to pump blood that contains oxygen and nutrients to over three hundred trillion cells in the body. It is scientifically proven that the average heart 'beats' (or expands and contracts) one hundred thousand times and pumps about two thousand gallons of blood each day. It is abundantly clear that if the physical heart malfunctions and stops providing oxygen and nutrients to the body, it automatically dies. Therefore, there are several bulletins and commercials that are warning us to protect our hearts from diseases such as coronary artery disease, endocarditis, hypertension, and congestive heart failure. If you don't take care of the heart by eating right and doing proper exercises, you are more vulnerable to be affected by one of these diseases, which could become life threatening.

Comparing the Spiritual and the Physical Hearts

Similarly, the Bible warns us *'Keep thy heart with all diligence; for out of it are the issues of life.'* (Prov. 4:23). The word 'keep' comes from the Hebrew word 'natsar', which means 'to watch, guard, or to preserve from dangers'. Hence you have a serious responsibility to watch, guard, or to preserve your spiritual heart from dangers because it is vital to your existence. I am reiterating that if you do not safeguard your heart, it can and will be exposed to dangers (pride, selfishness, perversion, lust, anger, depression, etc.), which could be detrimental to not only your spiritual health but also every aspect of your life.

If much anger, pride, and bitterness are in your heart, then you will be a dysfunctional person. Why? This simple analogy can clarify for you: a computer cannot function beyond what it is programmed to do. Similarly, if darkness is programmed in your heart, then you will function from a place of darkness. Remember that light and darkness cannot co-exist. In fact, if there is a storehouse of anger and bitterness in your heart, God does not even hear your prayer until you resolve those issues within your own heart. Therefore, it is vital that you do not clog up the communication line between you and heaven. You should always want to remain at a place, where there is constant communication (intimacy) between you and God. That is the best thing for you because it will bring insight and direction, which are critical for your spiritual nourishment and holistic growth in God's purpose.

Let us take a closer look at the spiritual heart. Why is the heart so important to *God?*

> The good man brings good things out of the good stored up in his heart,
> and the evil man brings evil things out of the evil stored up in his heart.
> For out of the overflow of his heart his mouth speaks. (Luke 6:45)

Heart comes from the Hebrew word 'leb', which literally means 'encompassing the inner man, mind, will, understanding, intelligence, knowledge, thinking, reflection, memory, appetites'. In Greek it's 'cardia', which similarly means the centre of affections, emotions, desires, appetites, and passions of man.

In essence, the heart is the decision-making headquarters of a man, encompassing his thinking, will, passions, appetites, memory, intelligence, and emotions. All of these factors are the driving force that compels the man

STANLEY R. SAUNDERS

to make decisions and function in the realms of the earth. The heart is the core of the inner man. Your heart is extremely important to God because if He can invade this area of your life, then the great reality of His nature and purpose can be birthed and expressed through you in unlimited ways. When people see you, they see God because we were created to be the expression of God in the earth. The more we can align our hearts with the principles of God's Word, the more we will be able to represent Him accurately in every area of our lives.

This is actually a lifelong process in which God wants you to engage. The more we allow Him in our hearts, the more room we give Him to work in our lives. I am excited about this process because I know that everything will work out for our good. Sometimes we are afraid to give up certain habits or tendencies, but as we trust God, we see and experience His salvation in unthinkable ways.

Imagine! If we had more men and women whose thoughts, feelings, beliefs, passions, and modes of operation were only reflective of God, the world would turn upside down because the sick would be healed, the blind would see; the prisoners would be free, Christians would be in harmony, marriages would be restored, the prodigal would come back home, and crime would decrease as love permeates the atmosphere of the nations. This would be better than walking on waters; it would be like soaring on eagles' wings because you will be in His perfect will. I believe that God is calling us to a place of heart surrendering.

He has diagnosed each of our hearts and found it to be so badly infected that the only solution to save us is to give us heart transplants. Well, the good news is that He will not only give us the new hearts but also will perform the surgery, and His hands are precise and perfect. Will you allow Him to work in your heart or do you have life all figured out? The reason He has allowed you to go through certain things in your life is that you are being perfected.

Capturing the Heart of God

The underlying purpose of this chapter is to help you arrive at the place, where you begin to desire the heart of God. As you capture His heart, you will be able to function from that place of purpose because you will be in tune with what God desires for your life in any given situation. It is one thing to say, 'God, I want to capture your heart'; however, it's another thing to actually put yourself in a position to be processed by God. When you put yourself to be processed, you are actually surrendering your will, desires, and emotions to God, and you exchange them for His will. This is not the easiest thing to do because many times we do not want to see things from God's perspective. God is calling us to capture His heart and do not be afraid to let go of our nearsightedness. God has already gone ahead and opened the necessary doors, but you need to trust Him and walk in complete obedience to His Word. Personally, I have come to realise that some of the very same things that I wanted to hold on to were not good for my life. God later revealed that to me.

When Bad Friendships affect Your Heart

There were two major times in my life when I had to make major decisions regarding friendships. In the first instance, I was in a backslidden state and was very far away from God at that time. I really sensed that God was calling me out of darkness, but my flesh refused to let go of the friends, because to me, they were my world. In brief, an incident happened when I was with those friends on prom night. We were 'hanging out' when a group of boys attacked us, and my friends sped away and left me. I felt betrayal for the very first time in my life. I then realised that if I continued along that path, it would lead to my destruction.

The reason I had to relinquish my associates was not so much the incident that had occurred, but the fact that my friends' influence was changing me. I was slowly transforming to become as they were. They were affecting my mentality and conditioning my heart to think a certain way. Therefore, I had to make the decision to follow God and change my association. This happened about eight years ago, and I am still serving God. That was a major change in direction for me. Looking back at it, I acknowledge that my heart was cold and wicked towards God, and I needed a wake-up call. Thank you, God!

When we are in the midst of certain situations, sometimes we feel like God is working against us. If we are not careful, those seeds of ill thoughts will grow in our hearts and cause us to rebel against God. I pray that we may never see God as an enemy but rather as the driving force behind every good purpose. This is the way we must condition our hearts. After God has shown us the condition of our hearts, we should embrace the next principle, which is called 'repentance'.

CHAPTER 4

The Two Sides of Repentance

'REPENTANCE' IS THE most powerful prerequisite for spiritual warfare. This is the door for entering and accessing the Kingdom of heaven on earth. Why? Let's examine the life of two important characters in the Bible: John, the Baptizer (the preparer of the way) and Jesus Christ (the Way). John the Baptist introduced the concept in the New Testament's Gospels. As a matter of fact, his entire ministry was based on the theme 'repentance': ¹In those days John the Baptist came, preaching in the Desert of Judea ²and saying, 'Repent, for the kingdom of heaven is near.' (Matt. 3:1-2, NIV)

Repentance was all that John preached! He spent a great deal of time challenging people to come to a place of repentance. John's message was very simple: if you do not repent, you will not inherit the kingdom of heaven. In other words, he was saying that man's access to God is weighed heavily on repentance. I really admire John because he preached repentance with such passion and determination; he spoke with a sense of urgency and was not afraid to boldly approach anybody.

Likewise, Jesus came on the scene shortly after and reinforced the same concept:

> ¹⁷From that time on Jesus began to preach, 'Repent, for the kingdom of heaven is near.' (Matt. 4:17)

The first words echoed out of the mouth of Jesus were not 'I love', or 'be blessed, my sons and daughters'. They were not 'You are more than conquerors', or 'peace be still'. Jesus made it abundantly clear what we need to do: *Repent.* Jesus emphasised this concept throughout the gospels. In fact, He died for that reason; His death gave man access to true repentance. In the same manner, Jesus stated that men ought to repent for the kingdom of heaven is near.

What is Repentance?

The word 'repent' comes from the Greek word 'metanoeo□', which means 'to think differently'. Jesus was essentially saying that in order to experience the fullness of God's kingdom on earth, our mentalities or mindsets need major adjustments. In brief, Jesus was saying 'Repentance is thinking how I think.' It is taking on, adopting, enforcing, marrying, embracing, and acculturating the mentality of kingdom in every area of your life, leaving no separation between church life and social life or any other life.

If you want to live for Jesus and represent His kingdom accurately on the earth, you have got to embrace the law and culture of repentance. The more you learn to think like Christ, the greater impact you will have. You are like a bomb waiting to explode. When you repent, it propels you into another dimension of thinking, where an unrepentant heart could never take you. You need to understand that your mentality is like a visa because having a visa determines what territory you can legally access. The more visas you have, the more territories you can explore. Therefore, the more you upgrade your mentality, the more territories you will conquer for the Kingdom of God.

Furthermore, as you begin to function like Him, people will begin to see God for who He is. They will no longer just be seeing the wickedness and corruption in the earth, but they will be seeing your lifestyle as a representation of hope in the midst of their situation. This is a serious challenge because it is easier to be like everybody else in the world. The easiest way to be revered and adored by the world is to go with the flow like everybody else. God is creating a distinct people! A distinct people are the ones who go against the flow. In other words, they break barriers: they break the norms and traditions, and, most importantly, their lifestyles speak volumes. A distinct people also hate sin with a passion because they want to please the King of kings. When you are in the Kingdom of God, you have a mentality that earnestly seeks to please your King, and every day that desire increases in you until it completely and intricately shapes and transforms your life.

Looking at different behaviours that are scripturally sinful, we can always trace them back to our mentalities. If you have a murderous mentality, it is only a matter of time before you eventually commit a murder. That is why Jesus said that if you even look at a woman with lust, you have committed adultery because in your heart, your intent is to sleep with her. Jesus is challenging mankind to change their wicked and corrupt ways of thinking. As we continue to explore this concept and examine our own hearts, we will agree that there are times when we get extremely angry and begin to think about wicked things to say or do.

If you reflect on it, you realise that whenever you find yourself in that place, you have to put those evil thoughts in check or else you will get out of control, right? The underlying principle here is that if you do not chastise a negative thought with a positive thought, those negative thoughts will be activated and get you into serious trouble.

There are many times when we try to block out negative thoughts and hope and pray that they will eventually go away. This is not the best approach because those negative thoughts will eventually resurface and intensify. The best approach is to confront such thoughts and deal with them once and for all. For example, if you struggle with fear, you must understand that God has not given you a spirit of fear. The only way to fight fear is by using faith. Therefore, you will have to feed your mind with any songs, Scriptures, books, ideas, and positive thoughts that will boost up your faith level, then you will experience a noticeable difference in your life. You need to confront negative thinking!

If you are struggling with some sort of sexual issues or habits, you need to come to grips with the truth that your body is the temple of the Holy Spirit and that sexual immorality will eventually destroy you. As you open your heart to the truth of God's Word, He will be able to intervene by His grace and deliver you from whatever situation you are facing. To tell you the truth, you cannot advance your life if you are not open to receive the truth. Repentance is like responding to God's knocking on the door of your heart:

> [20-21]Look at me. I stand at the door. I knock. If you hear me call and open the door, I'll come right in and sit down to supper with you. Conquerors will sit alongside me at the head table, just as I, having conquered, took the place of honour at the side of my Father. That's my gift to the conquerors! [22]Are your ears awake? Listen. Listen to the Wind Words, the Spirit blowing through the churches. (Revelation 3:20-22; The Message)

God wants to enter into your heart of hearts and cause a dramatic change in your life. But He will not force His way in. Will you invite Him in? He wants to dine with you! He wants to give you a new mentality! Will you allow Him?

The key principle in repentance is to change your mentality. We need to get rid of any old mentality that is not in line with the Word of God. I believe that God is calling us to a place, whereby we begin to hate sin with a passion and make some major adjustments in our hearts. We need to think differently and embrace the infallible truth of God's Word! It's not an easy thing, but we can do it! God says:

> My grace is enough; it's all you need.
> My strength comes into its own in your weakness.
> Once I heard that, I was glad to let it happen. I quit focusing on the handicap and began appreciating the gift. It was a case of Christ's strength moving in on my weakness. Now I take limitations in stride, and with good cheer, these limitations that cut me down to size—abuse, accidents, opposition, bad breaks. I just let Christ take over! And so the weaker I get, the stronger I become. (2 Cor. 12:9-10; The Message)

What is the Grace of God?

I once heard my pastor preach a sermon on the grace of God. He said that grace is the divine enablement of God. I had never heard it preached that way before, and as I examined the concept, it actually made sense. The grace of God is readily available to help us in our weaknesses. God says that when we are weak, He is strong. Regardless of where you are in your life, that same grace is available to help you whether you are a pastor, a politician, a drug addict, an altar boy, a priest, a young man, a millionaire, a young lady, or whoever you are. Isn't that amazing! God's grace is freely available to us, the humble and available vessels. It is the very thing that will help you overcome your struggles and difficulties. Tap into His grace. He will never disappoint you.

God has a flawless track record as a mighty deliverer and a warrior. I find it breathtaking that He is always working things out on our behalf. You are not the first person to have struggled, nor will you be the last. Shake off the dust and let the wisdom of the Word of God take precedence in your life. It's a guaranteed success! Are you ready to give Him your weaknesses? Are you ready to give up your struggles? Do you want to experience the unlimited grace in your life? What are you waiting for? God wants to show Himself strong in your life. Put Him to the test! He will make a way for you!

A Simple Prayer

If you are struggling in any area of your life, I want you to say this prayer:

Heavenly Father, I need you in my life. Thank you for your all-sufficient grace that is readily available for me. Help, God! Help me to overcome my_____. Give me the wisdom to make right decisions in regard to this area of my life. In accordance with your word, I declare that I am an overcomer, and I will make it through this time. Thank you, Lord, for your goodness and mercy that shall follow me all the days of my life. I give you praise, Oh Lord, for You alone are worthy. I give You all the glory and honour, in Jesus's name, Amen!

Dealing with Condemnation Once and for All!

As you allow God to work on your mentality and you continue to push yourself forward, you will have to fight through the issue of condemnation. Therefore, let's address the issue of condemnation with the truth of God's Word:

> [1]THEREFORE, [there is] now no condemnation (no adjudging guilty of wrong) for those who are in Christ Jesus, who live [and] walk not after the dictates of the flesh, but after the dictates of the Spirit. [2]For the law of the Spirit of life [which is] in Christ Jesus [the law of our new being] has freed me from the law of sin and of death. (Rom. 8:1-2; Amplified Bible)

Regardless of what you have done in your past, there is an assurance that God has freed you from that, and you no longer have to live your life with your head hanging down because of shame and guilt. Do not entertain thoughts of guilt because it will do you no good. If the Son of God has set you free, you are free indeed. There are times when we don't even want to forgive ourselves for something that we did years ago, but God is saying, 'I have forgiven you, my son. I have forgiven you, my daughter. It's time to move on, my precious child.'

I can hear Him saying, 'I am God! I don't live in the past. I am the God of now. My grace is here to propel you forward. Here are your wings! It's time to soar as the eagles, my child. No more believing the lies of the fowls, chicken, rooster, and turkeys around you. I am your God, and I have declared you are free from your past. Rise above every negative mentality and embrace what I am doing in your life, *my child*. I love you with an everlasting love. You are free! I have once and for all settled your debts with my precious blood!'

You are Aquitted!

What Does It Mean to be Acquitted? According to the *Merriam-Webster* Dictionary, 'acquittal' is 'to discharge completely (as from an obligation or accusation)'. *Dictionary.com* defines it as 'to relieve from a charge of fault or crime; declare not guilty: to release or discharge (a person) from an obligation; to settle or satisfy (a debt, obligation, claim, etc.); to free or clear (oneself)'. If a man were on trial for breaking the law, and the day before the sentencing the judge called him into his private chamber and said, 'You are acquitted', that would be the happiest day in that person's life. He would probably celebrate and dance through the streets with great passion and jubilation and shout, 'I am free! I am free!' He would not be ashamed of his freedom because he would remember what bondage was like. I am certain that that person would cherish his freedom.

The Other Scenario

In contrast to the person mentioned above, what if there was a person who was before the court, for whatever reason and the judge called that person into the private chamber and said, 'I know that you did commit those crimes years ago, and you should be sentenced to death, but you are acquitted. You are free to go home at this moment.' Then the person responds by saying, 'I deserve life imprisonment or the death penalty.' What would you think about that person? Most of you would call that person a lunatic or a victim of insanity. Why? A free man is expected to embrace freedom and act as a free man.

STANLEY R. SAUNDERS

The judge whom I spoke about is a representation of God, and the man who refused to walk in freedom represents a great number of people in the earth today. I am not just talking about people who are 'unsaved'; I am talking about 'saved' people who refuse to walk in freedom. The famous Bob Marley wrote and performed the song 'Redemption Song' in 1979, and it was later released in 1980 on *Bob Marley and the Wailers'* ninth Island music *album*, *Uprising*. I like this song because in truth, it represents the mentalities and lifestyles of so many people on the earth today. Why? One of the lines of a verse says to 'emancipate yourself from mental slavery'. From a historical perspective, slavery was abolished in the British colonies in 1834, in the United States in 1846, and the French colonies in 1848. The point that I am trying to make is that even though slavery was abolished years ago, Bob Marley believed that many people are still in bondage today. But the slavery that he was talking about is mental slavery.

Moreover, like the great artist, I share the same sentiment when it comes to the current mental state of humanity. It is my belief that a lot of people are wandering the earth aimlessly and feeling sorry for themselves because of what may have happened to them in the past. Maybe life did not go as they had planned or maybe they made major mistakes that are seemingly difficult to overcome. *Mental slavery is very destructive because it keeps you in the past; it tells you that you will never overcome your struggles and forever be a victim of your past.* Many people today believe this satanic lie. They actually believed the lies of the enemy and have become victims of mental slavery, without even recognising that they are actually in this state. This is not a good place to be because having the wrong mentality can destroy you in various ways, such as physically, spiritually, emotionally, financially, and socially. That is why we cannot afford to walk in condemnation but must learn to move from the past and be free.

The Truth about the Truth

To tell you the truth, Jesus died for us and put an end to spiritual slavery for all of humanity. Because of that great sacrifice, we are free from our past.

> [19]You will again have compassion on us; you will tread our sins underfoot
> and hurl all our iniquities into the depths of the sea. (Mic. 7:19)

We no longer have to walk around feeling sorry for ourselves; we can look forward to tomorrow with great expectation. If you have confessed your sins and asked for forgiveness, God has already cancelled that out; He does not hold your confessed sins against you. As a result, you have got to embrace your freedom with peace and excitement, knowing that God has already made a way for you. God revealed Himself to Moses as 'I am'. Now, I am talking about Moses, the murderer. I believe that when God revealed Himself to Moses as 'I am', it was symbolic that his past was dead; that is, whatever had happened in Egypt was obliterated. God was probably saying to His people that He had buried their past in Egypt.

It is comforting to know that God does not live in the past, and that is why He revealed Himself as 'I am'. The people of God were never instructed to turn back; they were instructed to go forward. The main problem that they faced was that even though they did not turn back geographically, they turned back in their minds and hearts. It seems to me that they were on merely a physical journey because their hearts were not connected to the living God, and they refused to let go of the old slavery mentality. Let's move forward in Christ and not go back to our old lifestyles. Amen!

The Other Dimension of Repentance: When Sin is not the Issue!

What is the other side of repentance? Personally, I see repentance as having two dimensions. Many times, when we think about the term 'repentance', we associate it with some sinful deed, such as sexual sins, violence, idolatry, gossiping, rebellion to name a few. Those are major sin issues, but the definition of repentance lends itself to what I describe as the other dimension of repentance: the 'sight-purpose' issue. Again Jesus said, '*Repent* for the kingdom of heaven is near.' Remember, the word 'repent' means to think differently or change your mind. This brings up some interesting questions: When do we need to think differently? When do we need to change our minds? Is it just when I am struggling with a sin issue? The answer is an emphatic no.

Let's further examine the life of Joseph and extract some key principles from his life. Remember that we looked at the life of Joseph and all that had happened to him, and we classified that as the 'Valley of Destiny'. Some of the things that happened to him include: His brothers were jealous of him; He was sold into slavery; Potiphar's wife lied about him, and he was thrown into prison. The word 'repent' means to think differently; therefore, the underlying principle of this terminology pushes us beyond the scope of sin. This means that God will allow us to face some serious situations that will require and demand that we think differently in order to bring forth His will for our lives.

The valley of destiny is all about God challenging you to think differently. It is a process whereby God begins to shape your mentality through hardships and trials. This is a strategic process that was ordained by God before the very foundations of the earth. It's the fiery furnace indeed because God uses the surrounding elements (your trials) to shape your mental psyche, which will enable you to become a greater representation of God.

What if Joseph, after he was sold into slavery, had spent months rebuking the devil out of his brothers? What if after Potiphar's wife had lied about Joseph, he had spent weeks and months rebuking the Spirit of Jezebel out of her? Would that have done him any good? In life, everything comes down to purpose. I once heard Myles Munroe say that if you do not know the purpose of a thing, you will abuse it. I believe that in Joseph's case, he had to arrive at a place where he began to trust God and embrace His purposes. The key principle here is that God is very interested in changing the mentalities of people. When we are in the valley of destiny, it forces us to start to think like God and see His purpose in the midst of a given situation.

I have discovered that even though we cannot stop the will of God, we can delay the plans of God, especially if we refuse to see things from His perspective. The wrong mentality or the wrong outlook of life can be very detrimental to your spiritual health. If you are not seeing things from God's angle, you can actually stifle the work of God. Remember, when God wanted Jonah to go to the people of Nineveh so that he would save the people by His grace, Jonah was very upset with God. He wanted God to destroy the people and that was not the purpose of God. In the case of Jonah, he was not in harmony with God, in terms of what God wanted at that time. Jonah had his own hidden agenda; he wanted the people dead. It is very important that we learn to think differently. Had Jonah learnt to think differently, he would not have functioned from a place of bitterness; instead, he would have embraced the purpose of God.

Unlike Jonah, Joseph really had to dig deep and trust God since, in the natural, slavery did not make sense. But he had to understand that slavery was just a temporary destination, not his final destination because God had bigger plans and places that He wanted to take Joseph for the purpose and advancement of His kingdom. Maybe, right now, you are facing a situation that seems like your final destination. However, I am writing this specifically to tell you that you need not believe the lies of the enemy. God will deliver you! The difficulties that you are facing right now are strengthening you for your promotion. Lift your head high and see the salvation of the Lord. Allow God to open your eyes so that you can see what He is doing in the midst of your trials. Ask God to reveal His purpose to you so that you can function accurately in the valley of destiny.

I believe that God is calling us, His people, to live a lifestyle of repentance, whereby we programme ourselves to think as He thinks. This is the best way to please God. If you are running a business organisation for someone, the best thing to do is to find out how the owner wants his business to function. You cannot understand the vision and purpose of the business if you do not consult with the owner. In the same manner, you are free to consult with the Lord (your owner) concerning your life so that you can have a clearer understanding of how He wants you to run your life, especially in these challenging times. I guarantee that as you make yourselves available, He will lead and direct you into the path of righteousness. You will no longer function from a place of confusion but from a place of peace and understanding.

CHAPTER 5

Who are You? Understanding the Power and Purpose of Your Identity in Spiritual Warfare

WHO ARE YOU? This is a question that is often asked whether it be directly or indirectly. If someone is knocking at your door, and you are not sure who that person is you might ask: Who is it? If that person's response is not satisfactory, I am certain that you would not give that person access to your home. Therefore, the identity of that person is the key to granting him/her access to your home because you don't want to expose yourself to possible danger.

A few days ago, I was at the bank trying to withdraw some money from my account, and the teller asked me for an identification card. After I had presented my card, she stated that the picture and signature were not clear. As a result, I had to present another identification card and rewrite my signature so that I could gain access to my account. Whenever you go to the bank and the teller asks you for an identification card, it focuses on one very significant concern: Who are you? When you are about to cross the border and the immigration officer asks you to present your passport and visa, it comes down to the same question: Who are you?

This question is extremely powerful because its response actually determines what you are able to access: your rights, privileges, benefits, inheritance, resources, etc. However, in addition to the benefits, it also outlines the roles and responsibilities that you must assume; these are more important than the tangible things. I have discovered that the world is in a serious state of anxiety and chaos because too many people are running away from their roles and responsibilities. For example, we have a great deal of men who just make children and refuse to take on the responsibilities of fatherhood. As a result, the earth is filled with a lot of children who are suffering from the 'disease' of 'fatherlessness'. Likewise, when these children become adults, they go forth and join the vicious cycle that continues from generation to generation.

Mankind is crying out for identity. People are doing some weird stuff in their quest for this. Sometimes people dye their hair different colours, pierce their bodies all over, change friends or social network, and even change their sex, all in pursuit of identity. I believe that God is longing to connect society to its rightful place of identity in Him, and the further we move away from God, the more distorted this image becomes. Why? If you have never discovered who you were designed to function like, you will always function from a dysfunctional place. Imagine a bird that never got the opportunity to fly because it thought it was a dog. What a tragedy?

God's Identification of Man

I now give to you a great 'tip', which you can apply whenever you are reading the Bible. Whenever God describes something, it is very important for us to get a deep understanding of whatever is the focus because there is eternal truth to it. I try to imagine God being in the designing room and taking His time to create man. One of the most powerful statements that He said regarding man is in Genesis 1:26-28:

> [26-28]God spoke: 'Let us make human beings in our image, make them reflecting our nature so they can be responsible for the fish in the sea, the birds in the air, the cattle, and, yes, Earth itself, and every animal that moves on the face of Earth.' God created human beings; he created them godlike, reflecting God's nature. He created them male and female. (The Message)

Let us study this very important passage of Scripture. In essence, God is saying, 'I have spiritually and genetically cloned myself in the form of man. Therefore, man has the inherent capacity to think and function as I do.' This is not a 'before sin' concept; this is an eternal concept. Imagine this! I am actually like God, that is, I have vast and limitless potentials that are waiting to be explored and harvested. Now, God-like identification and potentials are not good enough by themselves. The biblical message gives us a very clear understanding of the purpose of man's identification 'So they can be *responsible* for the fish in the sea, the birds in the air, the cattle . . . ' It can be concluded that the very purpose of discovering your identity is so that you can fulfil your earthly responsibilities. More than anything, I strongly sense that God is propelling His people towards a greater sense of responsibility. We have all the anointing, gifting, and heavenly resources, but, in general, we are not fully walking in a spirit of responsibility.

At the time of judgement, we will be judged according to how we assumed our kingdom responsibilities in the earth. Hence it is critical that we function from a place of obedience so that we can carry out the purposes of God in our environments. Let's face the truth: sometimes it is very challenging to walk in that reality! But more than anything, we need to stimulate ourselves to accept this reality. I have learnt that the more we challenge ourselves to do things, the more natural the activities become. The more you motivate yourself to become successful, the more natural and cultural it will become in your life. The more you practice prayer, the more natural it becomes. In the same light, responsibility can become contagious if we, the people of God, continue to exhibit it. If a light is shown in the midst of darkness, it has to have an effect on its surroundings.

Identifying Yourself in the Midst of the Valley

I have spoken at length about the two different valleys: the 'Valley of Bad Decision' and the 'Valley of Destiny'. I hope and pray that those of you who were trapped in the valley of bad decision have moved past that stage and are now beginning to function in your vocations (destinies). For those who are stepping into their destinies and are going through the trials and pruning of life, one of the first things that you have got to be reminded of is your identity in Christ. Often when things are not going our way, it is easy to lose sight of our identity. In fact, that is the number one tactic of the enemy. He constantly attempts to distort our image or our true identity in God. What do I mean by this? Whenever we find ourselves in an adverse situation, we notice that a lot of thoughts that produce negative emotions prevail.

Sometimes we feel frustrated, angry, worthless, disappointed, hopeless, etc. Now, these emotions can adversely affect our lives if we do not put them in check. When we function from any of these places, we are actually functioning from a place of false identity. For example, if a situation occurs in your work environment and you emotionally explode in front of your co-worker, your behaviour does not reflect the authentic you. Why? Hidden beyond those emotions is actually the image of Christ and any negative attitude and emotions that are not put in check can cause a false representation of that image.

In the case of Joseph, he had a lot of things that were seemingly going against him; but beyond the surface of those things was his identity. I believe the greatest thing that Joseph discovered in Egypt was not the riches of the earth or the power of prayer; it was his true identity in Christ. Joseph found his true self. As a result of that, he was able to function in Egypt and bring forth the purpose of God, in spite of the many circumstances that he was facing.

As I was studying the life of Joseph, it became very clear that he was a favoured child. The coat of many colours given to him was a stamp of identity—a mark of distinction. Many scholars believe that the robe was symbolic of royalty. Imagine, at age seventeen, he was given a mark of royalty! There was something beyond the scope of human understanding that his father saw in him. He saw destiny trapped in Joseph. Israel (Jacob) treated Jacob like kingdom-quality material, meaning that there was a God-ordained calling that must be fulfilled. So Joseph walked with that sense of purpose and carried the report back and forth to his father and pleased him. He also acknowledged his kingdom-royalty status, given that it was confirmed by the dream. Joseph walked with so much confidence that his brothers envied him and plotted against him.

What the valley of destiny did for Joseph was to help him rediscover his sense of kingdom-royalty. He somehow rediscovered his identity in a new light, and regardless of what he had been through, he did not lose sight of that. The discovery of that identity helped him to understand the revelation that I am imparting to you. The greatest lesson that God taught him was that identity comes with responsibilities. Therefore, Joseph walked in that revelation to the fullest extent. He was not only responsible on his job, but he also kept himself pure before God and remained blameless in the heat of troubles. He somehow became pregnant with the concept that he must bring forth the will of God, and he did it to the fullest and greatest extent.

You are Responsible to Bring Forth God's Will in the Midst of the Valley in Spite of the Way You Feel!

Emotions are like a roller coaster in that they go up and down and from side to side. You will never feel like you are at your best every day, but the eternal truth is that we are not governed by our emotions; it is the spirit man that is in charge. This is a very serious statement that we all need to get a very clear revelation of so that we can walk effectively in the earth. For example, when you are in the workplace and you are going through a difficult time, you need to first be reminded of your identity. Who are you? You are like God: This means, you have the capacity to think and function like God, and you have spiritual authority in the realms of the earth. So what then? So because you carry that identity you now have a Godly obligation to bring forth the purposes of God in the midst of that situation. It does not matter how difficult the situation is. All that matters to God is that you are bringing forth His purpose for that specific time and season.

Remember, the only reason we exist is to bring forth His purpose. God is purpose-minded, and He is constantly observing how we are doing in response to fulfilling our purposes. This is the reason that there is a constant tugging on our hearts. The pressures of life should never destroy or retard us. Our new philosophy should be more pressure, more purpose. As I evaluate my life, I realise that God has been using my most adverse situation as an opportunity for me to reach people in ways that I had never thought. I had a serious issue with a young man who was giving a lot of trouble in the classroom. So one day, I decided to call him aside and talk to him. After that conversation, I realised that he was facing tremendous issues. That was a divine opportunity to talk and minister wisdom into his life. Since that moment, I have seen a huge difference in his life. Many times, when we feel like everything is going wrong in our lives, it is a perfect opportunity for God to show us the possibilities of life.

When God allows you to go through the valley of destiny, He is actually testing to see how concrete you are in the identity that He has given you. I want you to note that the perception of one's identity is actually the foundation of one's values, character, thinking, and tendencies. How you see yourself will inevitably determine your values and subsequent behaviours. This is why Joseph did not fall for Potiphar's wife, and he remained connected to his God. It is impossible to function and succeed beyond the perception of your identity. Therefore, the discovery of your identity is one of the key ingredients to thriving in the midst of the valley. Once you discover or rediscover who you are, your thinking will automatically change in spite of your circumstances. You will not compromise in your thoughts or allow your emotions to control your life. This was the secret to the successes that Joseph experienced in Egypt.

I believe that God is challenging us to apply some of the same principles in our lives. You can do it! You can and will stand strong in the midst of the valley. God has given you the capacity to bring forth His purpose in the midst of where you are. Like Joseph, don't give up; instead, push yourself forward as the hands of the Lord are upon you. I guarantee you that, if you remain connected to God, He will show you more about yourself. You would be surprised to know what God will reveal to you. He will open your eyes to limitless possibilities. It's hard for me to explain, but you need to know who you really are. There is something that God is waiting to reveal to you about your true self. Don't take your identity lightly! You are very important to God. When God sees you, He sees an important figure. The Scripture describes us as vessels. We carry something that is important to Him. This is His purpose and plan. But I like to tell people this: it is not what you carry that is important; it is what you utilise to the fullest extent.

CHAPTER 6

The Power of Connectedness

THE OTHER DAY, I was trying to power my computer and it refused to start. I checked the other appliances in the home, and they also refused to power on. I immediately called a good family friend, who was an electrician. He came over to our home and began to trace the lines to determine what was causing the electrical problem. Initially, he said that the switch box and wiring needed to be changed. Therefore, we took him at his word, and we began to plan how we would get the necessary resources to rectify the problem. Before I made any purchase, I decided to consult another electrician. About a few hours later, he came to my house and began to trace the lines. He traced the lines way to the main source and found that there was a disconnection between the main line and the house line. He advised us to call the Belize Electricity Limited. I called the toll-free number, and a technician came and rectified the problem.

> [1] 'I am the true vine, and my Father is the gardener. [2]He cuts off every branch in me that bears no fruit, while every branch that does bear fruit he prunes so that it will be even more fruitful.' (John 15:1-2)

I want to highlight something from this Scripture that is very significant to the term 'connectedness', which means the act of joining or fastening together. When you are connected to something, a linking or a networking actually takes place, hence you move from a state of independence to dependence on the source of that thing. For example, an electrical wire is most useful when it is connected to the source of electricity. In other words, the value of the wire is in its connection to the source of electricity. Similarly, when you decide to connect yourself to the principles of God's Word, it is a very powerful resolution. You are actually declaring that you can no longer supply yourself with anything (physical, spiritual, financial, mental, etc.) and He (Jesus, the Word) is not only the reason for your existence but the source of your advancement. In addition, you are also declaring that your life is only as meaningful as your connection to the living Word (voice) of God.

You reach an awesome place of maturity, which is quite contrary to how the world operates. People have been declaring independence from family, spouses, systems of government, their jobs, etc. However, the principle of connectedness is actually your saying that 'regardless of what is happening, I desperately need my source (the Word of God). Accordingly, I also need to remain at a place of connectedness, or else I will never fulfil my divine calling on the earth.'

Let's look at the example that Jesus used in this passage of Scripture. The first important thing that Jesus did here was to establish His order of government. What do I mean by that? Jesus set the record straight. He was essentially saying that even though I am your source, my father is in charge of everything. That is a powerful statement. Many times, when we study this passage of Scripture, we 'run' at the fact that we will bear a lot of fruit, and so we get very excited about that.

The ultimate purpose of the connectedness is, of course, to bear fruit, but we need to focus more on what God wants us to do in order to bear to the maximum. It is very important to note that we cannot accomplish anything apart from God; we need a constant connection with God because this is the only means by which we would be able to communicate with Him and know what to do in any given situation.

I don't know about you, but I find myself needing to depend upon God more and more every day. Life is filled with a great deal of complexities, and the only way we can triumph victoriously is by constantly receiving and applying the wisdom of God, which comes as a result of connectedness. In order to experience the purpose and blessings of connectedness, you first have to understand God's hierarchy. Connectedness can only work for you if you apply its principles. We also need to understand that having connectedness today does not guarantee connectedness tomorrow.

If you have Internet access today, and you decide that you will not pay your bill next month, your Internet service provider will disconnect you, and you will lose your point of access. Therefore, the principle that all customers need to live by is called 'payment'. If the customers do not live by this principle, they will always find themselves in trouble with the source, which could lead to all sorts of problems. We can conclude then that connectedness in any sense is dependent on the individual's willingness to want to remain connected to the source. The individual's willingness is expressed in his/her desire to follow the laws/principles of connectedness.

The thing that is very important to note is that sources want to connect with individuals. For example, let's look at telecommunications for a minute. A number of telephone companies have been bombarding the public through the television, radio, Internet, billboards, etc. The only reason they have been doing this is that they want to increase their network by connecting with individuals all over the world. So we know that several sources of telecommunication are longing to connect with people. In fact, some companies have gotten so desperate that they are offering free phones, cheaper rates, unlimited access, unique mobile access, etc.

The principle behind all this is that even though these companies are investing a lot to connect with customers, they still cannot force the customers to be a part of their network. And even if the customers decide to join the network today, tomorrow they can decide to leave and go somewhere else. Let's further examine the principle of connectedness. In the same light, God cannot force Himself upon you. He does not function like that. You have to want to be connected to God and while you are connected to Him, you must have the desire to remain at that place. This will come through a sense of deep desperation and hunger to remain connected to God. This is a heart decision! God is calling humanity to a place of connectedness, but it is up to us to want Him.

God's Hierarchy: The Vinedresser Principle

Jesus made a very serious statement in the beginning of this Scripture: my Father is the vine dresser. Some other translation may say that Father is the farmer, gardener, or husbandman. What is it that we need to learn from this? First of all, let's establish in our hearts that the farmer decides what he wants to plant, uproot, prune, consume, replant, or even market. The gardener ultimately decides the fate of every living organism within the scope of his garden. What is the purpose of the gardener? The purpose of the gardener is simple: to do what he wants because he is the gardener. The gardener has an agenda in his heart as to why he wants to plant certain crops and when he will plant such crops. In simple terms, God has an idea (knows) in His heart as to what He wants to accomplish on the earth, and what He wants to accomplish through you. We are a part of His garden, and being as a part of His garden does not give us the right to dictate the will of God.

The gardener has the final say in all things, and that is the way how he functions. If I were to describe God in the context of this book, I would say that He is very 'will-centred'. I mean that He is only concerned about His will. This is not to say that God goes about like this big bully and bosses people around, but He is driven by His purpose, and He will never compromise His purposes. Just as the farmer plants a crop for a purpose, God has planted you in a particular garden (workplace, family, church community, nation, etc.) for a reason, and He is challenging you to remain connected so that you can accomplish that purpose. I know that things can be very rough at times, but your circumstances do not change the fact that God has a serious purpose that He wants to fulfil through you.

I think that we have to arrive at a place in our hearts, where we just allow God to be God, and stop analysing and rationalising every detail in our lives. Why? Let's look at this example. When a baker is making bread and puts all the ingredients in a bowl, everything looks chaotic to an onlooker. Furthermore, with just a glimpse at it, he may even think nothing good will come out of it. But as the baker continues to knead the dough, the more things begin to come together, so to speak. All the while, the baker knew what he was doing because he is the baker. In the same light, God knows what He is doing within the context of your life. Learn to just yield and allow Him to create His masterpiece!

Legal Obligation!

Looking back at the gardener, we need to note one of the most important things, which is that the gardener is obligated to attend to the garden. In the context of your life, you need to get a fresh revelation that God is obligated to you. Just as the farmer takes care of his crops on a consistent basis, God will do the same for you. A tree never has to worry about where its nourishment will come from; it knows that the farmer will take care. One of the other things that a good farmer does is that he makes sure the soil is of optimum quality. All that Joseph had to worry about was his connectedness with God. Sometimes we often question God and say, 'Why do you have me in this environment?' But rest assured that God has given you the right soil for your current environment.

The gardener knows what he is doing! You do not have to wrestle with God; it is His job to sustain you at any place in whatever valley of destiny you are going through. There is hope and nourishment available for you; you never have to worry for the gardener is in charge of the vine and the branch. Just as the gardener gets up early in the morning and waters the plant, God takes the same approach to provide for you all the time. I am convinced that we do not understand this fully. A true farmer thinks about more fruits all the time. You would be surprised that as I am speaking to your heart, God is also thinking about what strategies He would use to make you more productive. Think about that for a moment!

The Gardener is also Obligated to Protect the Garden

Apart from nourishing the plant, the gardener is also responsible to protect the garden. Many farmers have spent a great deal of moneys on herbicides and pesticides. The reason is that the farmers are aware that there are diseases and insects that have the potential to destroy the crops. Therefore, they would do whatever it takes to protect their investments.

> [17]no weapon forged against you will prevail, and you will refute every tongue that accuses you. This is the heritage of the servants of the LORD, and this is their vindication from me', declares the LORD. (Isa. 54:17)

I will not elaborate on this because it is a clear revelation that once you remain connected to God through your obedience and constant change of mentality, you do not have to worry about the devil. Why? It is a fact: Once you remain in God nothing shall, by any means, harm you. If you are connected to your phone company, and you are not in any arrears and something else is affecting your connection, the service provider is obligated to address that issue. Similarly, once you are connected to God, it does not matter who or what rises against you because God Almighty is obligated to take care of you. If God be for you, then who and what can dare to stand against you! Amen.

God's Hierarchy: The Vine Principle

Having examined the roles and responsibilities of the gardener, let us now look at the vine. Jesus describes Himself as the true vine in the Bible:

[1]I am the true vine, and my Father is the gardener. (John 15:1)

According to the Encarta Dictionary, a vine is 'a plant that supports itself by climbing, twining, or creeping along a surface.' In other words, a vine is the part that imparts nutrients to the branch, which enables growth and productivity. That is why a branch cannot bear fruits if it is disconnected from the tree. The very future of the branch is incumbent upon its connection to the vine. Let's look at it in another sense. Jesus also reveals Himself as the Word in the following Scripture:

[1]In the beginning was the Word, and the Word was with God, and the Word was God. [2] He was with God in the beginning. [3] Through him all things were made; without him nothing was made that has been made. (John 1:1-2)

Let us carefully examine the quoted text: Jesus (the Word) is comparing Himself to a vine. Accordingly, we need to study how a vine functions. First of all, it is because of the vine that the branches grow, but that is not the completion of the process. The same vine that causes the branch to grow is the same vine that nourishes it. The same vine that nourishes it is the same vine that flourishes it by enabling massive fruits to grow. Therefore, without the vine (the Word), it is impossible for fruits to grow. In the context of our lives, it is the applicable principles of the Word of God that will sustain and propel us through all the seasons of life.

Let me reiterate that you are nothing without the Word of God. You desperately need the Vine, which is your passport to achieving anything. The Words of God are absolutely real. I am not talking about quoting Scriptures. Before the beginning was, the Word was! Wow! So before there was ever a problem on earth, the Word was already the solution to the problem. Before any process had ever started, the Word was already the driving factor to complete all earthly, heavenly, and divine processes. For example, long before there were ever any sicknesses and diseases, the Word was already the solution to give health and soundness. God knew why He instructed that we should stay away from certain foods. They could be detrimental to our health; whereas, we have the Word to bring prosperity to our minds and body.

I have discovered something interesting about people. What you are actually looking for is not a religious experience; you want something that

STANLEY R. SAUNDERS

is tangibly authentic. In other words, you want to experience the realness of God's Word. This is what the Bible says about the Word:

> [12]For the Word that God speaks is alive and full of power [making it active, operative, energizing, and effective]; it is sharper than any two-edged sword, penetrating to the dividing line of the breath of life (soul) and [the immortal] spirit, and of joints and marrow [of the deepest parts of our nature], exposing and sifting and analyzing and judging the very thoughts and purposes of the heart. (Heb. 4:12; Amplified Bible)

This is a very dynamic passage of Scripture because it has so many powerful descriptions about the Word of God. First of all, let us reinforce a simple concept about the Word of God. The original intent of God was to have the Word in your hearts and not on paper. When God used to communicate with Adam, it was not with paper; they spoke face-to-face. The written Word of God is just to remind you about certain principles.

Some time ago, I was speaking to a group of young people about getting jobs or starting their own businesses. One young man, who was not working, came to me a few weeks after with a job application because he then wanted to apply for a job. I immediately took his application form and filled out a reference for him since I was so thrilled that he was applying God's Word (desiring to make the Word that mankind should work active). It finally made sense to him that the Word of God is real. His life was changed by what I had spoken to him.

People today, especially the young ones, want to experience something like that. I am telling you, a lot of times we underestimate the power of God's Word. The Scripture above says that the Word penetrates. That means where I cannot go physically, mentally, and emotionally, the Word of God can go. It did for the young man who decided to look for a job after I had spoken to him. The Word cut deep within his heart and caused a dramatic paradigm shift in his life. Undoubtedly, after he gets the job and applies the other principles of how to stay employed and be productive in the workplace, he will be fruitful.

On that same note, I was even more impressed with a young lady who came to me with a business idea. She mentioned that she wanted to start her own business and needed some assistance from me. Certainly, I would do my very best to assist her. But the whole point here is that the vine (the nutrients of God's Word) has the capacity to destroy old mentalities and bring forth change in the lives of people. As people of God, we should never underestimate the power of the Vine.

If you study how vines grow, you would understand that some vines grow up straight, some climb on walls, some climb underwater, some would grow across the highways, etc. My point is that vines will grow and anything that becomes connected to them will blossom. Anything built on the principle of the Word of God cannot fail! That is why you are destined to succeed. You have success written all over you because of the Word of God that is trapped within you. I encourage you to keep studying and applying the Word of God. It is bound to push you forward!

Do yourself a favour: Do not measure what God is doing in your life and compare it to what He is doing in somebody else's life. What God is building in each and every individual is unique! If you look at somebody else's life and compare it to yours, you might get discouraged. Sometimes, we do not know what God has rescued people from and we want to measure ourselves with them. We don't have to be jealous of people. All we have to do is to apply the necessary principles of God's Word and remember that there is always a due season for harvest.

When Joseph was in prison, it looked like nothing was being accomplished, but, amazingly, God had a plan for him. It is important to note that circumstances do not deactivate the power of God's Word because it is ever living. Therefore, it does not matter what you are going through; if you connect yourself to the principles of God's Word, you are bound to succeed. If you consider the trees of nature, you will note that they strive to stand tall even when natural disasters confront them. Isn't that amazing? That is why the Word of God says:

> ²But his delight and desire are in the law of the Lord, and on His law (the precepts, the instructions, the teachings of God) he habitually meditates (ponders and studies) by day and by night.

> ³And he shall be like a tree firmly planted [and tended] by the streams of water, ready to bring forth its fruit in its season; its leaf also shall not fade or wither; and everything he does shall prosper [and come to maturity]. (Ps. 1:2-3; Amplified Bible)

STANLEY R. SAUNDERS

God's Hierarchy: The Branch Principle

The branch principle is a powerful concept that we need to live by because this will determine the very outcome of our lives. I have visited many gardens in my life, and it is really a privilege to watch and enjoy God's creation:

> [1]THE [empty-headed] fool has said in his heart, there is no God. (Ps. 14:1-3)

When you look at creation and how everything fits together, how can you say that there is no God? God has created everything and made them fit together by the power of His Word. In John 15, mankind is compared to a branch. A branch can only fulfil its purpose if it is connected to the vine. In addition to that, the vine is compared to the living Word of God. As people of God, *we need to hate divorce with a passion.* We cannot afford to divorce ourselves from the principles of God's Word. It has already been prophesied:

> [5]I am the vine; you are the branches. If you remain in me and I in you, you will bear much fruit; apart from me you can do nothing. [6]If you do not remain in me, you are like a branch that is thrown away and withers; such branches are picked up, thrown into the fire and burned. [7] If you remain in me and my words remain in you, ask whatever you wish, and it will be done for you. [8]This is to my Father's glory, that you bear much fruit, showing yourselves to be my disciples.

This passage of Scripture has significant weight! It is similar to what God says in Deuteronomy 30:19:

> This day I call the heavens and the earth as witnesses against you that I have set before you life and death, blessings and curses. Now choose life, so that you and your children may live.

The secret to accomplishing the will of God is constant connectedness to the (Vine) Word of God. When you are in the valley of destiny, you especially need to connect to the Word of God. On the other hand, if you allow the bitter circumstances of life to disconnect you from God, you may even endorse the sinful act of aborting a baby. Don't get frustrated by what life throws at you! Instead, connect yourself to God at all times. For every chapter or season of your life, there is a different demand or requirement by God. It's like Jesus cursing the fig tree even though it was not yet time to bear fruits; He was still expecting something. Let's examine the story:

> [12]The next day as they were leaving Bethany, Jesus was hungry. [13]Seeing in the distance a fig tree in leaf, he went to find out if it had any fruit. When he reached it, he found nothing but leaves, because it was not the season for figs. [14]Then he said to the tree, 'May no one ever eat fruit from you again.' And his disciples heard him say it. [20]In the morning, as they went along, they saw the fig tree withered from the roots. [21]Peter remembered and said to Jesus, 'Rabbi, look! The fig tree you cursed has withered!' [22] 'Have faith in God,' Jesus answered. [23] 'Truly I tell you, if anyone says to this mountain, 'Go, throw yourself into the sea,' and does not doubt in their heart but believes that what they say will happen, it will be done for them. (Mark 11:12-14; 20-22)

We have the capacity to bear fruits in and out of season because the Kingdom of God functions differently from the world's system. At this point, I wish you, especially the young at heart, to pay keen attention to me. By the world's standard, it should normally take years for one to mature in certain areas of life (emotionally, spiritually, mentally, financially, etc.). Looking at this story with the fig tree, we see that there is a conflict happening here. This great conflict is what I call the battle of standards. Jesus is actually teaching His disciples to defy the world's standards of thinking and doing things. For example, in the natural world, it makes no sense to curse a fig tree, especially at that time. For years we have been taught that it should take you 'x' number of years to work and own a house or 'x' number of years to emerge into a great leader. God is prophetically speaking to you today! If you develop a love for His Word and abide in it, God will cause you to transcend time.

I believe that because we are in the last days and God is primarily concerned about establishing His kingdom, He (God) will surprise a lot of people. How? I believe that if we are willing to be used by God, which is measured by our obedience, His grace will explode in our lives. I believe that He will pour out His grace in unprecedented ways. For example, let's say that you desire to be used in a business that is God's will for you. We live in a time when there is a lot of darkness in the earth. Therefore, it has been prophesied that His light must shine in the darkness. What does that mean for you? If you apply the right principles outlined in the Word of God, I can't think of a reason why God would not use you in the business sector.

Why not you? I believe that it is your time now! We could actually curse or destroy anything; it could be as small as a fig tree or great as a mountain that would seek to hinder our progress in the earth. As people of God, we have to start believing that God wants to use us in every sector of society. God wants to use people in politics, law, business, engineering, education, hospitality, science, music, entertainment, and every other imaginable field. Therefore, I say to you again: Why not you? I want you to make a fresh commitment to yourself that you will continue to believe in the God-given capacity that you have. In addition, it is equally important that you continue to process your skills, talents, and your attitudes.

Be a Pioneer!

I know that God has been using numerous people in the different sectors of society to expand His kingdom. In my view, one person that has really stood out, especially over the past five years, is Tyler Perry. In Hollywood, he has been injecting the values of the kingdom, and many people have been touched by his work. His plays and movies address relevant issues that people are facing in their everyday lives. Hence people can identify with his shows, be entertained, and address key issues in their lives at the same time. I believe that he has been elevated because of his faithfulness and obedience to God's law. You can be like a Tyler Perry in your field of discipline. God can use you beyond your wildest imagination. Do you believe?

Moreover, the key thing here is that it takes a great mentality in order to defy all odds. I don't care what your family background is or what relatives and others have been saying about you. I am declaring that you can rise above the limitations of your ancestors and your fellow peers or countrymen. You will even soar beyond what your parents or teachers may have said about you. Don't take anything personal in regard to what your critics may have said about you because you will mount up with wings like eagles and rise above the norm. You will soar above the recession that is affecting so many people in the earth. Everything has to do with your mentality; that is why I love the parable of the fig tree so much.

God has called you a 'much-fruit' person! You have 'much-fruit' capacity trapped within you. God has only given the branch one simple responsibility, which is to abide in Him, meaning to apply the principles of His Word. In essence, He (God) will take care of everything else. You don't have to worry about getting wealth, accolades, respect, healing, status, clothing, shelter, finding a spouse, etc. Focus on applying the Word of God and that will be the pathway for all things. Isn't that awesome! The Greek word for 'abide' is meno☐ which means 'to stay, continue, dwell, endure, be present, remain, stand, tarry'. So in other words, the pathway to arriving at the 'much-fruit' level is to remain connected or married to the Word of God. No Divorce!

Don't Disregard the Earthly Gardeners!

People often like to think that they can just listen to God and don't worry about man. It is very important for us to remember that God has set up earthly authority as well. Let us study this passage of Scripture carefully:

> [1]Let everyone be subject to the governing authorities, for there is no authority except that which God has established. The authorities that exist have been established by God. [2]Consequently, whoever rebels against the authority is rebelling against what God has instituted, and those who do so will bring judgment on themselves. [3]For rulers hold no terror for those who do right, but for those who do wrong. Do you want to be free from fear of the one in authority? Then do what is right and you will be commended. [4]For the one in authority is God's servant for your good. But if you do wrong, be afraid, for rulers do not bear the sword for no reason. They are God's servants, agents of wrath to bring punishment on the wrongdoer. [5]Therefore, it is necessary to submit to the authorities, not only because of possible punishment but also as a matter of conscience. (Rom. 13:1-5)

According to the above, God has a high level of respect for earthly authority. As a matter of fact, we can certainly conclude that He is the one who has allowed authorities to be there in the first place. Let's draw another conclusion: It is impossible to say that you will connect yourself to God, but you will disregard earthly authority. It does not matter how smart you are or what degree or qualification you have. God doesn't care about those in that sense. What if your boss or husband is not a Christian? Well, you still need to submit to him because that person represents the authority and the order of God on earth. When you disrespect any authority, you disrespect God; therefore, your level of connectedness is affected. In short, those who are disrespectful towards leaders (earthly authority) are spiritually malfunctioning. This also suggests that they are in darkness and their relationship with God is affected. What do I mean? When people are at this place, they are not in obedience to God's Word and have created a barrier between man, God, and themselves. Notice that when people are in conflict with leaders, productivity is stifled. Why? If you don't trust and respect somebody, you will not work hard for him/her. Your sense of loyalty will be non-existent and you will not bear much fruit in the workplace or any other environment.

In my humble opinion, one of the greatest signs of spiritual maturity is how you relate to the leaders around you. God will always test us in this area. I was thinking about Joseph's life. He was a very humble young man because he never disrespected Pharaoh or Potiphar. He served his leaders with all diligence. When you are submissive to authority, it is easy for God to elevate you. Why? People are always taking notice of how you respond to certain situations, and if you have proven to be prideful, nobody will come to you for counsel. This was Joseph's ticket to the top. Had he been disrespectful to authorities, he would have spent his entire life in prison or even ended up dead.

David was another great example. Remember that King Saul tried to kill him. David spent years running for his life, but he remained humble, and God elevated him in the right time and season. I always tell people this: humility is your ticket to promotion. God wants to exalt His people. If you have been struggling in this area, God is calling you out of darkness into His marvellous light. It's time for us to step up kingdom-living so that the world can see the glory of God.

I have discovered that whenever you humble yourself before God, He only has one choice but to elevate you. In fact, it's important to note that humility attracts God. He is very near to the humbled and far away from the proud. A lot of born-again believers are struggling with this concept. There are many people who are wrestling with earthly authority. Some people don't want to listen to their husbands, their supervisors, parents, teachers, etc. What does this have to do with spiritual warfare? Whenever you are at war, with your leaders (figures of authority), it creates disunity. We need to understand that God cannot function where there is disunity; consequently, the work, will, and purpose of God are stifled.

CHAPTER 7

Pruning: The Pathway to Greater Connectedness in Spiritual Warfare

A S I WAS studying this passage of Scripture (John 15), it became very clear to me that in order to produce much fruit, there is a necessary process. This is called 'pruning'. In order to embrace this process, it only makes sense that we first understand the purpose of it. Now, many times, the focus is on what we want to accomplish in life. For example, we may want to start a ministry or do a lot of great things for God. But too often, we want to run away from pruning, which is our pathway to greater purpose and accomplishments. Let us look at John 15:1-3:

> ¹⁻³I am the Real Vine and my Father is the Farmer. He cuts off every branch of me that doesn't bear grapes. And every branch that is grape-bearing he prunes back so it will bear even more. You are already pruned back by the message I have spoken.

As we focus on the passage of Scripture, it is important again to note God's order of government. Now we need to understand that the very same God who decides what He wants to plant is the very same God who decides what He will prune. It is important to walk in this understanding because the very purpose of pruning is to bear much fruit, and the more fruit you bear is an indication of the level of purpose in which you are walking. Therefore, if no pruning takes place, then you will retard growth and stifle the purpose and plans of God. I have discovered that the more effort we make to bring forth the will of God, the more we will live to please Him. God enjoys when we manifest lifestyles that are pleasing to Him because, in this case, He gets the glory. The more we obey God, the more people see Him for who He really is.

What is Pruning?

Pruning is the act of trimming or the removing of what is not needed. As a gardener scrutinises a tree, he decides what needs to be removed and then embarks on that process. He is basically removing what is not required from the plant. I am sure that when you are cleaning your house, you would remove the dust on the television because it is not required. If you leave the dust in your home, you could be affected by allergies, cold, and asthma, not to mention the damage it does to the television and other equipment in your home.

In the context of the plant world, pruning also removes plant diseases. As a result, if you do not prune that diseased area, it can spread to the other parts of the plants and cause greater damage. That is why the farmer has to take his time and carefully cut away the diseased stuff. As soon as the farmer cuts them away, the plant automatically begins or increases its fruit bearing process. This indicates that it is at a better place after pruning.

In the context of your life, pruning could be the cutting away of mentalities, habits, attitudes, practices, opportunities, or even people that hinder God's purpose for your life. I know you might be thinking, '*Why people?*' Well, to answer that, I would say that a lot of times God would cut away some of the people who are a hindrance to your development. Sometimes we hold on to people and relationships that God wants to subtract. If we are not careful about whom we associate with, they can frame our thinking and limit our growth. I am not talking about Christian and non-Christian people because even some Christian friends can be a hindrance to our lives. Therefore, we have just got to yield to what God is doing in this area because He knows best.

Many times, when God wants to remove things or people from our lives, we do not see how they are negatively affecting us. It comes as a result of this preconceived notion: We know best for ourselves. Unfortunately, sometimes we take that same attitude to the workplace, into our marriages, church community, etc. We have to be very careful with this attitude because by nature, as human beings, we are very rebellious and proud. If God does not intervene with His pruning hands, we will get out of control and grow like wild trees that are more vulnerable to diseases. That is why God has to take the scissors and cut away these nuisances from our lives.

Furthermore, it does not matter how long you have been walking with God, pruning applies to mature trees as well. In fact, let me state that no tree is exempted from pruning. Similarly, none of us is exempted from this process because we have not yet reached full maturity, and there is more growth to be experienced. I have found a passage of Scripture to further explain. Let's look at Proverbs 25:4:

> 4Take away the dross from the silver, and there shall come forth [the material for] a vessel for the silversmith [to work up].

The gardener is also like a silversmith. A silversmith is a *craftsperson* who makes objects from *silver* and/or *gold* (Wikipedia). The word 'dross' is actually referring to scum formed on molten metals, usually caused by oxidation (Encarta Dictionary). Whenever you find a piece of gold or silver, there are usually a lot of scum and impurities found on the minerals. Therefore, the silversmith has to purify it. When people go to the store and purchase a piece of jewellery, it is usually in a pure state. What a silversmith has to do in order to remove impurities is to heat up the metals. The more heat is applied to the object, the more purified the metal becomes, which affects its value, quality, usability, and even beauty.

In the context of our lives, God is the silversmith. In order to remove the impurities from our lives, He has to apply heat. How does He do that? Sometimes He allows us to go through certain types of adversities. If you notice, when you find yourself in certain situations, much pride, anger, bitterness, and frustration surface to the top. Many times, you may even surprise yourself and say, 'I did not know that I was like this. From where did this anger come?'

Sometimes God will allow your boss, your teacher, or your spouse to prune you. I know that this is not your typical prosperity message, but that is just how God operates; He uses the foolish things to confound the wise. The good news about all this is that when all these impurities surface to the top, it is an opportunity for God to remove all the impurities from your life. It is His time to take away all the excess baggage from your life. This is a very good time for you! You might not enjoy the feeling, but eventually it will all work out for your good.

Do You Trust Him?

At the end of the day, you have to be willing to trust Him:

⁵Trust in the LORD with all your heart and lean not on your own understanding; ⁶in all your ways submit to him, and he will make your paths straight. (Prov. 3:5-6)

Do you trust God? This is a serious question. Do you trust that He is moulding you into a better person? Many times, we find ourselves wrestling with this truth, especially when things are not going the way we had planned or expected. When you say, 'I trust in you, God,' it's a serious statement. When you trust the bank you put your entire savings in it. Most people, who have money, do not put their finances in their home because the home is not safe; therefore, they trust the bank because it is the safest option.

They believe that when it is time to withdraw, their monies would be there. They also believe that the bank will offer all the benefits such as interests, convenient transactions, loans, etc. That is trust! Most people believe that. Nobody ever expects that when he/she goes to the bank, his/her money will be lost. That is trust! Nobody believes that when it is time to collect interest he/she will not get any interest. That is trust! In addition, a person who trusts will always give because both terms are synonymous. Let us refocus on the bank scenario, as an example. We give them our monies because we trust them. People share private information with others because of the trust factor.

Let us apply Proverbs 3:5-6. What is trust? It is the reliance on the integrity, strength, ability, surety, etc. of a person or a thing. In the context of our lives, trusting would be to secure or give everything, including our finances, dreams, and deepest desires, as well as what we think is right, what we think is wrong, and even what we don't understand to God. This is supposed to be done with no conditions attached or no secret or hidden agenda. In other words, you give God everything because it is the right thing to do and because He is God, and there is nothing else you would rather do than to please God. That is the place to which God is calling us.

We cannot achieve anything without first trusting God. In fact, I would go as far as to say that trusting in God is the prerequisite for any advancement in your life. If you don't trust in Him, you will depend on some other source for help. The problem with that is that anything built apart from God will not have a lasting impact. It will be like the man who built his house upon the sand—we all know what happened to him. It is also my belief that when you truly trust in God, you deny ownership of everything and embrace stewardship. That is, you demote yourself from owner to steward. When you own things, the pressure is on you to protect and provide. But when you steward something, the pressure is on the owner to take care. That is why it is best to trust (give and secure) everything to God because He is a good owner with a proven track record of excellence.

Let's Look at another Definition

Another definition for trust, which I find to be interesting, is to 'hie' for refuge. The word 'hie' literally means to go somewhere in a hurry or to cause yourself to go quickly. In reference to what we are talking about, it would simply mean to constantly seek God as your refuge, with no hesitation. When we are doing business with God, we have to be careful not to hesitate. When you hesitate, your trust becomes vulnerable, and this can make you spiritually destructible. What does this mean? When you delay your trust, a lot of negative thoughts could potentially bombard your mind, and the longer you stay in this process, the more susceptible you are to spiritual diseases such as pride, discouragement, fear, frustration, and anxiety. Whatever situation you are facing, you should be in a hurry to apply the principles of God, who is your refuge and strong tower.

You don't want to contract any of those spiritual diseases; that is why trust in God is defined as 'to come to Him in a hurry'. If you hesitate, you might believe the negative report of your doctor. If you hesitate, you might believe that the people of God are in a state of recession. I can just hear God saying, 'Just trust Me because I will not disappoint.' Trusting in God requires no understanding! What does this mean? All that is required here is movement towards God. If you wait for understanding, it may never come. Sometimes, as human beings, we want to know the beginning, end, and all the 'in-betweens'. Many times, God does not reveal all those details to us; therefore, we have to rely solely on His reputation as God, omniscient and omnipotent.

At other times, we spend a great deal of time worrying about what has been lost or what could be lost? Therefore, we spend a lot of energy and time trying to analyse life, using our own intellectual faculty and reasoning. However, God is saying that all of that is not important. Just go to Him in a hurry and He will take care of all the rest. David describes God as a refuge and a strong tower. The men of old would use a tower primarily for safety and to look at the strategies of the enemy. God is like a strong tower because in Him, we are safe. We need to get rid of the fear! God will not harm us or allow anything to harm us! You can trust everything to Him, who has an eternal track record of faithfulness. It is His nature to do you good in spite of your circumstances. The following is one of my favourite Scriptures:

> [19]God is not human, that he should lie, not a human being, that he should change his mind. Does he speak and then not act? Does he promise and not fulfil? (Num. 23:19)

This makes trusting easy! God has a great history of awesomeness. The Scripture says that God is not a man. What is that saying? He has no weaknesses, no limitations. He does not hold grudge. He shows no favouritism. He is not abusive. He does no harm, and He will not disappoint. God is stuck with you! He is forever obligated to you by virtue of your existence on earth. God has good thoughts towards you and nothing will change His perception of you:

> [11]For I know the thoughts and plans that I have for you, says the Lord, thoughts and plans for welfare and peace and not for evil, to give you hope in your final outcome. (Jer. 29:11; Amplified Bible)

I believe that God has a prosperity plan for you and He has indebted Himself to complete this plan; however, the completion of the plan is dependent on the trust factor. Do you trust Him to complete this plan? Will you remain committed to Him in the midst of your valley? I want you to think about these questions as you continue to journey in Him.

In All Your Ways, Acknowledge Him, and He Shall Direct Your Path!

When you acknowledge something or someone, it is a high form of respect. The Scripture says that we are to acknowledge Him in all our ways. One of the meanings for the word 'acknowledge' is 'to designate or to appoint'. This is a very powerful revelation: in everything that we do, God needs to be appointed before He acts. Remember that God has given us the gift of free will, which means we have the power to choose or refuse. Therefore, if He is to become responsible for you, you have to appoint Him as Lord of your life. Sometimes we appoint Him, but at other times, we demote Him from being Lord of our lives. When we do this, it creates not only a stronghold of instability in our lives but also a lukewarm temperature. That is why sometimes we are on fire for God, and at other times, we are in deep hibernation like bears.

I believe that God is once again knocking on the door of your heart. He wants to be appointed as King in your life; He wants to reign in your heart at a deeper level. Oftentimes, He has no appointed position in our hearts; therefore, we treat Him disrespectfully even when we are in the midst of our crises. If He is appointed as your 'nothing', then there is nothing that He can do in the midst of events or a given situation in your life. I am challenging you to once again designate Him as Lord of your life. Designate Him as your source of everything because He has a track record of faithfulness.

He Will Make Your Paths Straight

Finally, the Scripture says that He will make your paths straight. What does this mean? The word 'path' means a well-trodden road; this has a lot to do with your sense of direction. Therefore, what God will do here is to bring a greater sense of direction and alignment in your life. In other words, the things that are inaccurate and out of order, would now be corrected in your life. As humans, we tend to forget something very interesting about God: He knows everything. The Scripture says that God knows the beginning from the end *(Isa. 46:10)*. Let us now examine another text that I find interesting:

> ²Looking away [from all that will distract] to Jesus, Who is the Leader and the Source of our faith [giving the first incentive for our belief] and is also its Finisher [bringing it to maturity and perfection]. He, for the joy [of obtaining the prize] that was set before Him, endured the cross, despising and ignoring the shame, and is now seated at the right hand of the throne of God. (Heb. 12:2; Amplified Bible)

The fact that you are alive is a clear indication that God has a prosperous life ahead for you. If you are not clear about what to do, then the best thing to do is to consult the One who created you to do His good pleasure. I spoke earlier about appointing or delegating God in all things. When you do this, God will bring you to a great place of accuracy and purpose. You will have peace in your heart, knowing that you are trotting on the right path even if everybody else thinks that you are insane. Remember, when Job's wife told him to curse God and die, Job refused to do that. Instead, he captured something internal that propelled him forward to the end. When we obey God's Word, we always have to assure ourselves that God will never lead us on a destructive path. The end result will always be good: it will always be to further advance His kingdom.

Gold in Your Valley

There is gold in your valley! Many times, when we are at the lowest place in our lives, we do not focus on the gold because all we see are impurities. Spiritually, God is scraping the scum from your eyes; He is pruning you because He wants to make you more usable. You might be saying, 'Why am I going through this or that?' All God is doing is making you more usable in your environment so that you can become more productive in the expansion of His kingdom. Remember that God is always testing your response.

God knows about your talents and gifting. God does not care about your talents because those are given. He is in the business of character development. God knows that if He can develop your character, He can then get the most out of you. This is a work in progress; many times, we want to shape our own characters or images. But I believe God is calling us to a place of surrendering to Him. This is a place at which we allow Him to shape and mould us into His character or image. Pruning is the pathway to that! We need to trust God because He knows what He is doing.

Oftentimes, when we are facing the pressures of life, we tend to ask ourselves the question: Where are you God? Let me tell you something! When God is cutting, it does not mean that you are not in the presence of God. In fact, let me announce that when He is cutting and shaping, it's a clear indication that you are in His presence because He is at work within you. He is pushing you toward a more productive state. When the farmer wants the tree to bear more fruits, he prunes it. That is what God is doing right now through your valley. It is very important that we remain connected to God so that our hearts do not rebel against this process. Imagine what would have been the outcome if Joseph had spent months just fasting and rebuking the devil. What would that have done to him? It might not have done him any good.

Moreover, connectedness gives us insight into the plans of God. It gives us a sense of hope that God is at work in spite of the circumstances. I also see it as a form of a spiritual mirror, whereby God is showing a split image.

One of the images is the image of God, which is perfect and complete. The other image is that of yourself, journeying towards completion. This journey is a movement towards maturity. I am not saying that you will not make mistakes, but as you mature, you learn to make better decisions and function better in the realms of the earth.

One of the main reasons God is working on our mentality is that it determines the extent to which we would go to see the Kingdom of God increase in the midst of our world. What if God tells you to do something differently, such as approach people differently, see people differently, talk to people differently, love people differently? What would be your spiritual, mental, emotional, and social responses to such? The answers to these would definitely determine where your heart is. Let's look at this passage of Scripture:

> [18]But forget all that—it is nothing compared to what I am going to do. [19]For I am about to do something new. See, I have already begun! Do you not see it?
> I will make a pathway through the wilderness.
> I will create rivers in the dry wasteland.
> [20]The wild animals in the fields will thank me, the jackals and owls, too, for giving them water in the desert.
> Yes, I will make rivers in the dry wasteland so my chosen people can be refreshed.
> [21]I have made Israel for myself, and they will someday honor me before the whole world. (Isa. 43:18-21; New Living Translation)

Please take some time to study this passage carefully because there are some very powerful revelations in it. Let me challenge your mental faculty! God not only says that He is going to do something new, but He has also already begun. Therefore, if I am to function accurately in the realms of the earth, I must buy into the philosophy of God. What is the philosophy of God? God's philosophy is that His people need to become convinced of what He has started. What has He started? He has started to expand His kingdom in the hearts of His chosen people and has committed Himself to finishing that project. When you remain connected to God, you will see and know exactly what He has started and wants to finish in your life. The thing about this is that He will show you specifically what to do, if you have an open mind (a mature mind).

The greatest evidence of being connected to God is a renewed mentality.

> [17]Therefore, if anyone is in Christ, the new creation has come: the old has gone, the new is here! (2 Cor. 5:17)

A new mentality is the only thing that can kill the 'old man', which represents the fleshly carnal (selfish ungodly) ways of doing things. The phrase 'in Christ' is also referring to a state of continuous connectedness to Christ (the Word). Let me prophecy to you! If you allow God to prune you, you will go to places that are beyond your wildest dream. Let's look at Moses. While Moses remained connected to God, he was never confused. When the people of Israel were in the desert and they were thirsty, God gave Moses the solution in spite of their very displeasing behaviours that caused him (Moses) to encounter much stress.

> Go out in front of the people. Take with you some of the elders of Israel and take in your hand the staff with which you struck the Nile, and go. [6]I will stand there before you by the rock at Horeb. Strike the rock, and water will come out of it for the people to drink. (Exod. 17:5-6)

God gave Moses a specific and critical instruction to follow. **In the realms of our natural understanding**, striking a rock for water makes no sense. Indeed, Moses had to follow an instruction that required a renewed mentality. For every instruction that God gave Moses, he had to upgrade his mentality in order to facilitate what God wanted for that specific time and season. Look at your life! Whatever God is telling you to do right now requires a new mentality. What are you going to do about it? Stop running! Will you take on that new mentality or will you hide in a cave? Are you even seeing what God is seeing or are you afraid? Why are you afraid? Trust in the Lord and He will make a way for you.

God has a Problem with Mediocrity!

Why does God have a problem with mediocrity? 'Mediocrity is a quality that is adequate or acceptable, but not very good' (Encarta Dictionary). This is my philosophy: If you have the capacity to be average, then you can be good; if you have the capacity to be good, then you can be very good; if you have the capacity to be very good, then you can be excellent. Mediocrity is a curse; it is not from God. If you go back to Genesis, you read that when God was creating the earth, He was making comments about His handiwork. Whenever God made something, He said that it was good. Do not be deceived by the word 'good'. This word means 'pleasure'. Therefore, whenever God created something, He was saying that it was pleasurable to Him. In other words, His creation is up to His standards, which is one of excellence. Accordingly, God is calling a people to rise up to that mentality and begin to make a remarkable difference in their world. It's a serious challenge.

One of the easiest things to do is to settle at a place where you are comfortable. I am not saying that there is anything wrong with comfort, but at times, comfort leads to mediocrity. When I was playing basketball, the coach would say that I needed to learn to use both hands. To me, that was very uncomfortable. I had difficulty doing that at first. Then when I slowly learnt to use both hands, I became a better basketball player because my ability to score increased.

We must condition our minds to do whatever it takes to rise above the norm. Think about this! The world is already dark, and it will continue to increase in wickedness and corruption. In addition to that, a lot of people are suffering in many ways. So then, why not stand and make a difference? Why not you? Let us remain connected to God and make a bold stand for Him. Now is the time to start moving. We want to kill the 'old man' and take on the mentality of a warrior.

In 1 Peter 2:9, God made a very serious statement regarding His people:

> But ye are a chosen generation, a royal priesthood, an holy nation, a peculiar people; that ye should shew forth the praises of him who hath called you out of darkness into his marvellous light.

What I comprehend from this passage is it is a fact that God has not only given us a kingdom identity, but He also has set a standard. For example, He said through Peter, 'that ye should shew forth the praises . . . 'The word 'praises' in this context means *manliness* (*valour*), that is, excellence (Greek dictionary). This passage excites me because it declares that God has equipped

STANLEY R. SAUNDERS

us for excellence, and He is now demanding it from us. We have no excuses because excellence is in our spiritual DNA. We have everything it takes to produce excellence in the midst of every given season that life presents. Let us now move forward with this mentality!

PART B

Understanding Your Weapons and Keys to Connectivity

CHAPTER 8

Keys to Stand Victoriously in the Midst of the Valley

THE PREVIOUS TWO chapters speak a great deal about the principles of connectedness, which are the passport to fruitfulness, and the keys to sustained victory in spiritual warfare. What we want to do now is to examine some of our weapons (connectors) that will enable us to become established in the purposes of God. Remember that the underlying principle of connectedness is that we become able to bear much fruit. However, we cannot bear fruit if we are not connected; therefore, we have to battle to remain connected or else we will never experience any lasting victory in our lives. Let us examine the following passage of Scripture:

> [10]Finally, my brethren, be strong in the Lord, and in the power of his might. [11]Put on the whole armour of God, that ye may be able to stand against the wiles of the devil. [12]For we wrestle not against flesh and blood, but against principalities, against powers, against the rulers of the darkness of this world, against spiritual wickedness in high places. [13]Wherefore take unto you the whole armour of God, that ye may be able to withstand in the evil day, and having done all, to stand. [14]Stand therefore, having your loins girt about with truth, and having on the breastplate of righteousness; [15]And your feet shod with the preparation of the gospel of peace; [16]Above all, taking the shield of faith, wherewith ye shall be able to quench all the fiery darts of the wicked. [17]And take the helmet of salvation, and the sword of the Spirit, which is the word of God. (Eph. 6:10-20; King James Version)

One of the first things that is established here is the position that God is calling us to assume in the realms of the earth. God is exhorting His people to take up a position of strength: *be strong in the Lord and in the power of his might* (Eph. 6:10). The term 'be strong' comes from the Greek word 'endunamoo□', which means 'to empower, equip, enable, (increase in) strength'. Paul is making a very serious statement here. The empowerment and equipping that you need in order to survive in this world can only come through Christ Jesus. By this, I mean that we must embrace and apply the Word (principles) of God, which will propel us forward at all times in our daily lives.

God is calling us to live at a place of constant empowering and equipping. I like to call this a place of desperation and dependence upon your source (the principles of the Word of God). We are supposed to be living at a place, whereby we have this mentality that we cannot go on without *God*—our source of everything. Therefore, your strength is dependent on the measure by which you are applying God's principles in your life. When a person is weak, the cause can always be traced back to some principle that he/she has violated. For example, when David went on the roof and saw the woman bathing, he subsequently pursued her and violated the principle of righteousness.

Next!

The other part of that Scripture says, 'And in the power of his might' (Eph. 6:10). It's very important for us to note that the word 'power', in the preceding context, means 'dominion'. Therefore, the above passage is saying that if we learn to live by the principles of God's Word, it will create an atmosphere of dominion within the context of our world. This is all about having the right mentality about the living Word of God. The writer Paul is essentially telling us to catch the right mentality at all times since it will be the decisive key to our success, by bringing us to a place where we reign regardless of the circumstances facing us.

Moreover, the problem that a lot of us have is that we have been taught to trust our intellect. What happens when you don't have the answers? What happens when you no longer have the strength to go on? As human beings, what we need to do every day is to have a great celebration! What are we celebrating? Every day, we need to celebrate our declaration of dependence upon God. This is not a position of weakness or inferiority but rather a position of power (dominion) because when we are weak, He is strong. We cannot do anything in our own strength; His Word is the key, the enabling factor.

Why Do We Need Weapons?

Whenever somebody carries a weapon, it's a strong indication that he/she is trying to protect something or someone. A trained soldier carries a weapon because he needs to protect a particular territory for a specific purpose. Most soldiers have a sound understanding about the history and the value of their country or territory. Why? You will not die for something that you do not value. That is why soldiers are initially taught to value their country. In fact, when an individual enrols in the army, that person is, basically, sacrificing himself/herself for the greater good of the country. That is why some countries invest billions and trillions of dollars in their military, and they are constantly seeking to expand their army base. It's all about gaining stronghold over territory!

In the context of the war, in which we are engaged, it is also about territory. Paul has instructed us in Ephesians, Chapter 6 to 'Put on the whole armour of God.' So then, the two important questions that we need to answer are: What do we need to protect? Why do we need to protect? If we are not able to answer these questions, then we will never be effective in spiritual warfare, and we will function from a place of inaccuracy. Again, Myles Munroe said, 'If you don't know the purpose of a thing, you will abuse it.' I believe that a lot of believers have been abusing the weapons of spiritual warfare. Furthermore, Dr. Myles Munroe also defines 'abuse' as 'abnormal use'. Therefore, we can be doing something that is spiritually good; but, at the same, we are still functioning from a place of inaccuracy, Wow! That is interesting.

Let me bring a great sense of clarity to you as it relates to the 'Armour of God' and the instruction given by the Apostle Paul. If you study Ephesians 6 carefully, you will realise that Paul uses the word 'stand' multiple times. One of the meanings for the word 'stand' is 'to be established'. The Scripture puts it in context: 'So that we may be able to stand against the wiles of the enemy.' We have to be very careful how we interpret this portion of Scripture. Let me bring some serious revelation to you again. The objective of spiritual warfare is not to kill the devil or his demons! Please note that people have been praying and fasting for centuries. If the objective of spiritual warfare were to kill the devil and all demons, don't you think that they would have been dead by now?

Moreover, it's time for a paradigm shift! As the people of God, we need a 'mental makeover' because if we don't change our way of thinking, we will never have a lasting impact on this generation. To tell you the truth, a lot of people do not see the church as a relevant entity because the church is, for the most part, still trying to kill the devil and his demons; in addition to the fact that we spend a great deal of time fighting each other. Consequently, we need to refocus on our primary kingdom objective, which is to stand or be established on the earth.

We need to realise that while we are attacking each other's doctrinal beliefs, darkness is subtly establishing itself in the realm of the earth, and the Scripture has prophesied that it will also increase. What are we going to do about it? This is a question whose answer needs to be resolved within our hearts because we will never be at peace with ourselves and God if we don't make a difference in our world. Likewise, God will hold us accountable for the territory that He has given us. Therefore, one of the greatest things that we need to understand in order to fulfil our earthly mandate is called the 'principle of establishment'.

Establish What?

I know that you are asking yourself, 'What do we need to establish?' What we need to establish, especially in an adverse situation is the 'right mind'. We need to learn to see adversity as an opportunity rather than a tragedy. The beauty about a right mentality is that it is the open door to producing the purposes of God. As human beings, we are like incubators, always carrying the purposes of God on the inside. The only thing about this is that many times we quit and never end up birthing the purposes in our God-assigned communities. What a tragedy? Whenever you give up or hide, you allow the works of the enemy to prevail and conquer. The battle between the spirit and the flesh is a battle for the mind. Whichever is in charge (the spirit or the flesh), at any given point in time, will overcome. That is why Paul says that we are to crucify the flesh:

> But put ye on the Lord Jesus Christ, and make not provision for the flesh, to fulfil the lusts thereof. (Rom. 13:14; KJV)

The above Scripture says that we are to make no provision for the flesh. The word 'provision' is literally translated as 'forethought', which means planning or plotting in advance of acting, or premeditation (the Free Dictionary). Please note that the 'flesh' is basically any pattern of thinking, which is contrary to the principles of the Word of God. In paraphrase, this passage of Scripture is saying that if we entertain negative thinking, our thoughts will take root and decide our future. In essence, negative thoughts that are continually encouraged will slowly and viciously inhabit our minds and stifle the purposes of God.

Moreover, a warfare mentality (the right mind) produces a breeding ground for God to manifest His will in any given situation. That is why it does not matter what are the circumstances and situation that you are facing. All you need to do is to capture the right mentality and be rooted and established in that which is the prerequisite of any breakthrough. The lack of this is the reason Jonah disappointed God when he wanted the people destroyed. Having the right mind, in Jonah's case, would have made him say honestly, 'God, I have issues with these people, but I am willing to submit to your plans for this city. Give me the grace to push forward and love just as you love.' In regard to whatever challenges you are facing, I emphasise that you always need to establish 'the right mind', which is the key to kingdom advancement. You might not understand all the fine details; but, if you are willing, you can always ask God to help you establish the right mind.

Furthermore, for that same reason, God chose David in spite of his frailties:

> And Samuel said to Saul, Thou hast done foolishly: thou hast not kept the commandment of the LORD thy God, which he commanded thee: for now would the LORD have established thy kingdom upon Israel for ever.
>
> [14]But now thy kingdom shall not continue: the LORD hath sought him a man after his own heart, and the LORD hath commanded him to be captain over his people, because thou hast not kept that which the LORD commanded thee. (1 Sam. 13:13-14; King James Version)

The key principle here is that if your thinking patterns are continuously synonymous with God's thinking patterns (His Word), then God considers you a man after His own heart and His kingdom—to manifest His desire for the earth. That is a big deal for God. Similarly, that is why our hearts and prayers must always be to seek God's face and to please Him.

The Right Mentality is the Sweet Fragrance of Worship

I often hear pastors talk about how worship is like a sweet smelling fragrance unto God. Why is that? I spent years asking myself this question. Worship goes way beyond the context of a song or the lifting of hands. I would personally define worship as 'having a sacrificial mentality'. What do I mean by this? Whatever the act of worship is—be it kneeling, bowing, giving, and lifting of hands—it first requires a sacrificial mentality. A sacrificial mentality is simply a divine exchange of mentality by which you are actually trading your thinking patterns in exchange for God's thinking pattern. For example, when you sacrifice 'your' mentality, you will undoubtedly praise Him; sing a new song unto Him; dance before Him; kneel before Him; bow before Him; give to His kingdom.

When you grasp the mentality that He is God, regardless of what circumstances you are facing, then your expression towards God automatically produces worship. As a result, anything you do in response to the fact that He is God becomes an act of worship unto Him. But remember that everything starts with having the right mentality. I am telling you that if we can capture the right mentality, then we would turn our world upside down for the kingdom.

I sense, more and more, that God is challenging His people to a place of accurate thinking and decision-making. When the woman poured her expensive perfume on Jesus, that was worship. She somehow got the mental revelation that He is the King of kings and deserved all of her worship. When Abraham was dragging his son to the altar in an attempt to execute the will of God, it was also worship. How much are you willing to sacrifice to see the will of God manifest in your life? This is a serious question!

STANLEY R. SAUNDERS

CHAPTER 9

Understanding the Weapon of Prayer in Spiritual Warfare

GOD HAS BEEN teaching me, especially over the past five years, a great deal about prayer. I believe that every kingdom endeavour needs to be initiated by prayer. In the realms of the kingdom, nothing should be done without it being preceded by prayer. Why would Jesus spend countless hours praying before He executed His daily activities? Why were His prayers effective? Why do we need to pray? These were some of the questions that have been plaguing my mind for years. I know that the subject of 'prayer' has been taught and written about a great deal, but my personal search for truth began because of my frustrations.

I was frustrated because I did not understand the significance of prayer. It was not working the way I wanted it to work! Most people spend hours pushing an agenda before God. To be honest, I was one of them. As a matter of fact, my frustration was particularly stirred when God did not meet my agenda. How did that affect me? It affected me to a great extent because my perception of God was tainted. I began to think about God merely as 'Maybe He might answer my prayer, or maybe He may not answer my prayer.' It's important to note that the intensity of the prayer life of most people is dependent on how God meets their perceived needs; therefore, most people have this tendency to measure and relate to God based on how God responds to their perceived needs. A 'perceived' need is what a person believes that God needs to address in a particular situation, based on his/her assessment of God, self, and the problem(s).

What is Wrong with That?

The more I study about the Kingdom of God, the more I am growing in the revelation that 'it's not about me'. One of the greatest revelations that I have understood is that even when faced with adversity, one is the least important person, yet one can have the greatest impact. For example, when Jesus was in the Garden of Gethsemane, He got the revelation that His Father's will was more important than His life. That was a serious place of maturity for Him. As I continue to study the life of Jesus Christ, I learn that He never intentionally drew attention to Himself, and He accomplished all that His Father wanted. His very lifestyle was pleasing to God.

Remember that when Jesus was in the Garden of Gethsemane, He concluded His prayer by making a very serious statement: 'Not my will but yours be done.' That was the highlight and climax of His prayer life. Then, after He had made that statement, an angel of the Lord came and strengthened Him, and He finished His course. As soon as He got that revelation about prayer, God's grace was ready to meet and propel Him forward. Now, Jesus had an effective prayerful lifestyle!

Effective Prayer Supersedes the Boundaries of Merely Talking to God

Is talking to God enough? I once heard a pastor define 'prayer' as simply 'talking to God'. I am not saying that this definition is 'way off track', but based on what I have learnt, it goes way beyond the scope of merely talking to God. In my humble opinion, the greatest question that needs to be clarified is: What do we need to talk to God about? The answer to this question will ultimately determine how we relate to God. Imagine that an influential billionaire wants to endeavour in real estate development, and he is seeking out trustees to manage his corporation. Imagine that he has heard so much about your potential and sets an appointment to meet with you regarding his strategic operations.

What if in the meeting, the billionaire came with his strategic plans and objectives, but he never got the opportunity to present them to you. He did not get the opportunity to make his presentation because you came with your own strategic plans and objectives. What do you think would be the outcome of that meeting? Now, you had the opportunity to be in conference with the billionaire, but the meeting was not productive—it was a waste of time. Consequently, the billionaire will not entrust you with his corporation because you have your own philosophy and hidden agenda.

What's the Point?

Prayer is very simple! The billionaire investor whom I told you about represents God. You are the trustee who is very important to the investor. He wants to expand his real estate corporation. As an executive employee, your conferencing with the investor is solely business. Any conversation that is not related to his agenda is simply a waste of time; therefore, when you do not carry out the objectives of the investor, and/or delay the plans of the investor, you could lose your status with him. Please note that your response to the investor should not be taken lightly. It is critical that you discipline yourself so that you can carry out his agenda. Likewise, if the agenda of God, your investor, is to be manifested, then you the trustee must execute the plans of your investor. All your investor cares about is His agenda (His kingdom).

God created you for a specific purpose. Regardless of what is happening around you, there is nothing that can cancel that purpose. Therefore, it is important that you learn to develop a prayerful response to the time in which we are living. Effective prayer is all about putting yourself in a position to constantly receive the agendas of God with an understanding that you are expected to carry out those agendas, regardless of the circumstances of life. When you are in the valley of destiny and things seem not to be going your way, it is easy to fall into the temptation of wanting to push your own agenda forward. Let's refer to Joseph as an example. As we continue to look at the life of Joseph, it is important to note that God had an agenda for him even when he was in prison. I am sure that there were many nights when he wanted to leave Egypt, but he had to be spiritually aware, in his heart, that he was at the place to disregard his agenda and execute the agenda of God. That is maturity!

In the Cool of the Day!

The main purpose of payer is to connect with God so that you can execute His will. It's interesting to note that Adam and God had such a close and natural relationship that the word 'prayer' was not even mentioned. That deep level of interaction was so natural that there was no need to name it. I believe God designed prayer to be second nature. It's ridiculous how we have things all backwards. Most of the times, we plan and then we pray to

God, and we see this as a spiritual thing. It is supposed to be done in the opposite manner. All your planning is supposed to come from a position of prayer because how will you know what to do if you don't consult the boss. It is important to also note that God did not intend for us to struggle to make time for prayer. If prayer is second nature, then the challenge lies in making time for other things. I believe that God is once again calling us to connect with Him at a deeper level, but this will require great trust and sacrifice. What happened to the time when you were really excited to connect with God? What went wrong? Why aren't you excited again?

God Knows Best! Do You Really Believe This?

Unfortunately, many times, we don't see things from God's perspective, and we end up pointing fingers at Him. Prayer connects you to a great place of insight. I believe that whenever you make God's agenda your priority, He begins to entrust you with more authority and responsibilities. This is usually challenging because God often leads us to a place that, in the natural, does not seem to make any sense. When the children of Israel were on their way to the promise land, God led them to a strange place:

> [23]And when they came to Marah, they could not drink of the waters of Marah, for they were bitter: therefore the name of it was called Marah. [24]And the people murmured against Moses, saying, what shall we drink? (Exod. 15:23-24; King James Version)

These people had a very strange response to God. They did not respond by seeking God's face; they responded by murmuring and complaining against God. Remember, this happened just after God had parted the Red Sea. I believe that our first response towards God should always be: 'Lord, what do you want me to do?' However, most of the times, our first response to God is usually, 'God I want you to do xyz . . . because abc . . .'

What if God does not want to meet your xyz? That is why it is important to seek His face. We need to learn to spend time in the Word of God so that it can sharpen our sense of awareness as to what God wants done. The more we spend time in God's Word, the more it creates an awareness of purpose in our lives. That is why the Bible says that the Word is active. Whenever you input the Word of God in your life, it becomes the active, guiding voice that leads you to the path of right decision-making. I can recall that a famous song says, 'The Word of God speaks . . . ' Accordingly, we can conclude that if we are to fulfil our earthly assignment, it is imperative that we develop an active prayer life so that we will know how to function in every situation that life presents.

Teach Us How to Pray, God!

'Lord, teach us how to pray, just as John taught his disciples . . .' (Luke 11:1). This statement is as important as the instructions or pattern given to the disciples. Why? I am not certain which one of the disciples made this statement, but I assure you that he made this statement because he saw desirable results in the life of Jesus. In general, people want to learn because they have either experienced or have seen the importance of a thing, and they want to apply it to enhance their lives. As disciples of Christ, it is chiefly important that we develop a teachable spirit, which is the prerequisite for any growth and further advancement. When the disciple made that statement, Jesus was ready to impart life-changing principles of prayer.

In reference to prayer, it is very important to note that there will always be room for growth in this area because praying is all about hearing and applying: the purpose of hearing is so that you can apply. A lot of times, we get too preoccupied with the hearing aspect and we neglect the application process, which is the heart of God. If you have the right mentality, God is willing to help you mature in this area. However, it must be something that comes from deep within you. If you desire to grow in prayer, God will give you the desire of your heart. As a matter of fact, His heart will become your heart as you become one in His will. Let us now look at some key components of the prayer pattern that Jesus outlined in Matthew, Chapter 6 and Luke, Chapter 11. The first thing that Jesus does here is to address God as the Father. Why is that important?

Keys for Effective Prayer: Our Father!

Wow! God is the Father of fathers. The more I read the Word, the more I understand about the Father—heart of God. Imagine this: God numbers the tears that we shed *(Ps. 56:8)* and He even knows the number of hairs that is on our heads *(Luke 12:7)*. It just shows how detailed our heavenly Father is concerning our lives. There is nothing about our lives that is insignificant to Him! God cares so much about us that I cannot adequately express the love of God in writing or in speech. This passage of Scripture is challenging us to relate to Him as a Father who cannot fail. He is committed to His Word and His reputation as 'Father God', so He never lies:

> God is not a man, that he should lie, nor a son of man, that he should change his mind. Does he speak and then not act? Does he promise and not fulfil? (Num. 23:19)

We need to learn to relate to God as someone whom we can trust! I am not talking about a conditional trust, but rather a lifestyle of relating to Him as our personal Father. When we picture God in our minds, we need to have this fixed image of a faithful, unfailing, living reality that is available to us. Having this mentality, you will definitely make your prayer life relevant because you are now seeing God as the source of everything. In addition, regardless of what you are facing, it will not deter you from seeking His will for your life.

Prayer
Father, I know that a lot of people are struggling to relate to you as a father. I pray that you teach us how to trust you as the unfailing God. I also pray for the fatherless that you would begin to heal all wounds of rejection, hurt and bitterness. I also pray that our men would rise up and assume the role of fatherhood and mentor this youthful generation. Let your will be done in the earth! I ask all this in Jesus' name. AMEN!

Keys for Effective Prayer: Hallowed be thy Name

> Let them praise the name of the LORD: for his name alone is excellent; his glory is above the earth and heaven. (Ps. 148:13; King James Version)

Many people today do not understand the Hebrew concepts of names; consequently, without adequate research, they end up selecting any name for their children. In the Hebrew culture, parents would carefully and prayerfully choose the names of their children because they believe that naming a child is linked to the destiny of the child. In fact, there are several accounts in the Bible, whereby God intervened in the naming or renaming process. For example, Abram was renamed to Abraham, Sarai to Sarah,

STANLEY R. SAUNDERS

and Jacob to Israel, to name a few. The word 'name' in the Hebrew speaks of the nature, quality, character, fame, honour, authority, and reputation of a being.

In Lester Sumrall's book, *The Names of God*, he explains that when you are calling the name of a person, you are declaring the God-ordained destiny of that person. I think that, if I may use this example, he is implying that if a child's name is translated as 'greatness', whenever you call that child's name, you are referring to him as a great person. Therefore, in the Hebrew culture, parents took pride in the naming of their offspring. This is a significant concept because I am thinking that even when you are upset with your child and some sometimes yell at him, the spiritual concept is still in effect.

How About God?

If we apply the 'name concept', the same can be said about God. In the Old Testament, God revealed Himself to His servants in many ways:

- *El Shaddai* (Lord God Almighty)
- *El Elyon* (The Most High God)
- *Adonai* (Lord, Master)
- *Yahweh* (Lord, Jehovah)
- *Jehovah Nissi* (The Lord My Banner)
- *Jehovah-Raah* (The Lord My Shepherd)
- *Jehovah Rapha* (The Lord That Heals)
- *Jehovah Shammah* (The Lord Is There)
- *Jehovah Tsidkenu* (The Lord Our Righteousness)
- *Jehovah Mekoddishkem* (The Lord Who Sanctifies You)
- *El Olam* (The Everlasting God)
- *Elohim* (God)
- *Qanna* (Jealous)
- *Jehovah Jireh* (The Lord Will Provide)
- *Jehovah Shalom* (The Lord Is Peace)
- *Jehovah Sabaoth* (The Lord of Hosts)

All of these names represent the unblemished reputation of God. Therefore, what Jesus was teaching His disciples was that when they prayed they must not cease to relate to God, based on His track record of greatness.

These names also vindicate the nature and fatherhood quality of God. For example, we should regard Him as a provider, healer, sanctifier, shepherd, master, etc. It is important that we download an image of His reputation in our minds and heart so that when we approach Him in prayer, we come boldly and expectantly, for this will boost our faith level and transform our mentality. As kingdom citizens, we need to grow in relating to God from the perspective of who He is.

He is Unchanging!

The reputation of God will never change: God will never stop loving; God will never stop providing; God will never stop healing; God will never stop being God. When we understand this about God, it does not matter what circumstances we are facing. I find it amazing that the average believer spends most of the time talking about his/her struggles rather than focusing on the principles outlined in the Word of God, who is able to help him/her to overcome any problem.

Imagine that you have a mechanical problem and the mechanic is right beside you, but instead of entrusting your car to him, you spend hours telling him about your woes. You spend hours telling him, 'I don't know how I am going to fix this car. This problem is impossible to fix.' Can you imagine how the mechanic will feel, given that he is fully qualified to help you with your problem? This is the lesson that we need to learn: We need to stop approaching God as if He is incompetent and believe that with Him, all things are possible. In this prayer pattern, Jesus is simply saying that we ought to look to God as a competent king who is fully qualified to solve all problems.

Keys for Effective Prayer: Thy Kingdom come. Thy will be done on earth, as it is in Heaven . . .

I think that the average born—again believer spends too much time focusing on heaven. Today, there are numerous songs written with heavenly emphasis. If heaven were the objective, then why would Jesus devote His entire ministry teaching us about how we should live on the earth? If going to heaven was God's objective, then He would have killed you after you had gotten saved.

STANLEY R. SAUNDERS

⁶My people are destroyed for lack of knowledge: because thou hast rejected knowledge, I will also reject thee, that thou shalt be no priest to me: seeing thou hast forgotten the law of thy God, I will also forget thy children. (Hosea 4:6; King James Version)

Often we approach prayer without any understanding of the concept 'kingdom'. Besides, God has given us a prayer pattern because His kingdom is His chief priority. If we are to live righteously for Him, then His priority must become our priority. Furthermore, we cannot honestly say that we love the things of God when we still have conflicting priorities deep within our hearts. I often hear people quote the statement: 'Let your kingdom come on Earth!' This should not be a circumstantial declaration but rather a fixed mentality that needs to invade the very depths of our hearts. Our hearts must begin to crave deeply for the Kingdom of God at all times.

I humbly believe that there is a deeper expression of the Kingdom of God, waiting to be birthed. Moreover, it will not birth forth until you grab a hold of it and pray it through. Evaluate your prayer life! Whatever you spend most of the time praying for is obviously your priority. You cannot say that the Kingdom of God is chiefly important to you; yet you spend countless nights praying for another job, merely because you are 'fed up' with your work colleagues. That position is not reflective of a warfare mentality; it comes from a selfish and fearful mentality.

Let me define this statement: 'Let your kingdom come on earth!' The word 'kingdom' means 'to rule or reign' and the word 'come' is translated in English as 'come forth', 'show itself', or 'be established'. Therefore, in your prayers, your heart should desire the reign of God in the hearts of a people. In addition, it is important to note that you are also putting pressure on yourself. Why? In order for God to reign in the midst of your circumstances, He first needs to reign in your heart. You have the power to determine the extent to which God is revealed in the midst of your community. Your earnest and heartfelt prayers are vital! According to what Jesus is saying in Matthew, Chapter 6, it is evident that the Pharisees had a consistent prayer life. However, it is clear that their prayers were chiefly in vain because they did not take time to seek the kingdom.

The Kingdom is Always Buried in the Valley of Destiny: Prayer without Ceasing is the Heart of the Kingdom!

In 1 Thessalonians 5, The Apostle Paul made a very serious statement that we desperately need to understand so that this principle can govern our lives:

> [16-18]Be cheerful no matter what; pray all the time; thank God no matter what happens. This is the way God wants you who belong to Christ Jesus to live. (The Message)

Other translations use the term 'pray without ceasing'. What is important to note here is that the term 'without ceasing' means uninterruptedly. In other words, your prayer life is not supposed to be measured by what you are going through. You have a serious responsibility to not allow anything to slow down the momentum of your prayer life. Likewise, we should not allow seasons to determine how we respond to God in prayer. As people of God, we need to be very careful to guard our hearts against religion because religion dictates that we will pray to God at designated times, e.g., on/in certain days/seasons. But God's kingdom is primarily about a lifestyle rather than a routine. In relation to prayer, Jesus has given us, in His words, some solemn commands that we need to follow:

> ALSO [Jesus] told them a parable to the effect that they ought always to pray and not to turn coward (faint, lose heart, and give up). (Luke 18:1; Amplified Bible)

> [5]If any of you is deficient in wisdom, let him ask of the giving God [Who gives] to everyone liberally and ungrudgingly, without reproaching or faultfinding, and it will be given him. [6]Only it must be in faith that he asks with no wavering (no hesitating, no doubting). For the one who wavers (hesitates, doubts) is like the billowing surge out at sea that is blown hither and thither and tossed by the wind. (James 1:5-8; Amplified Bible)

When you pray without ceasing, you create an open avenue for God to invade your community. It's a form of invitation for Him to release His grace and power divinely in the midst of your world. This is why I believe that whenever we stop praying we dishonour God. Why? We need to get the revelation that through our prayers we are actually birthing the kingdom. That's a powerful role! I beseech you not to take this lightly, my brothers and sisters. Your prayers are the only avenue through which God can work for you. Therefore, when you get frustrated and quit, you are, unfortunately, delaying kingdom activities. As I earlier stated, the reign of God is manifested only in the hearts of the people. That is why God says:

> [14]If My people, who are called by My name, shall humble themselves, pray, seek, crave, and require of necessity My face and turn from their wicked ways, then will I hear from heaven, forgive their sin, and heal their land. (2 Chr. 7:14; Amplified Bible)

Life is very simple. If you have a heart for prayer and you hate sin, then you can do kingdom business with God. It does not matter what the circumstances are because God is willing to heal. Maybe you are going through a rough time, but in the midst of that God can bring a dimension of wholeness into your life. In fact, I believe that He wants to bring wholeness into your environment. However, the only way in which we will see the manifestation of that is by holding relentlessly in prayer.

In light of the above, I encourage you, my brothers, and sisters, to hold steadfast in prayer and see the salvation of the Lord. Even though we live in a world affected by much negativity, our prayer life keeps us charged with great hope. When you commune with God, you will inevitably reap hope because God speaks good news. And even if He chastises you, it will be for good. Naturally, the key to walking in joy and hope is to develop an active, aggressive prayer life. This is kingdom behaviour that God requires and assists us in establishing within our hearts.

There is Room for Petitions too!

I want you to consider the fact that God also responds to petitions. In the realms of the kingdom, we do not petition with a selfish intent. In simple terms, a petition is a request made unto a higher authority (e.g., a king). A petition is granted based on constitutional rights only. Therefore, the power of your petition is in knowing your constitutional rights. For example, a trained attorney can defend someone whose rights are being violated. In the realms of the kingdom, Jesus is our attorney. When we petition unto Him, He takes the case before our Heavenly Father. The reason you always have a good case in Christ is that He not only knows the law (Word) but He is also the Law (Word). Consequently, when He (Christ) presents your case before

God, He is actually presenting Himself before God because we are in Christ. That is why when your petition in Jesus's name is emanated from the right heart, God cannot help but to grant you justice (answered prayer).

Is it wrong to pray for things? No, there is nothing wrong with that. Let me explain the concept of asking in this way. When you ask God for things, the heart is supposed to be saying, 'Lord, Grant unto me so that I can be in a better position to help others.' Nothing in the kingdom ever stops at an individual's level. There is always a corporate or community emphasis with God. Consider this! Why would you ask God for a job or a business? If God gives you a job or a business, you would be able to not only provide for yourself or your family but also help society. How? You have essentially put yourself in the productive sector of society; hence the welfare system does not have to worry about you and your family. Secondly, if you work or have a business, you will also contribute to society through the means of taxation.

In addition, you will also get the privilege to pay your tithes and offerings to the Kingdom of God so that the gospel of the kingdom can be further preached in every sector of society. Then, you also get to contribute to society by being a model citizen after whom people can design their lives. You can even hire people, depending on the size of your business, and lessen the unemployment rate in your community. Ladies and gentlemen, that is the power of kingdom-petition because it crosses the boundaries of self-interest and services the purpose of God's kingdom. Furthermore, that is why God promises that when we seek His kingdom and His righteousness, He will add all other things we desire. So then there is nothing wrong if you want to ask but don't forget to seek and knock.

Keys for Effective Prayer: The Power of Intercession

I want to share with you a revelation that I have gotten about prayer. Let me reintroduce you to another level of prayer that is very effective. Are you ready to move up to another level? Whenever they are going through trials, most people tend to focus primarily on themselves. Sometimes a person may cry out, 'God, get me out of this situation because I am struggling and I cannot take it anymore.' That is usually the position that most people take, especially when faced with a difficult situation.

I believe that most people spend 95 percent of the time praying for themselves. What is wrong with that? I believe that when people focus

STANLEY R. SAUNDERS

primarily on themselves during prayer, it creates an atmosphere of selfishness, which is anti-kingdom. At this point, let me tell you about the type of prayer that catches God's attention and moves Him. When you pray this type of prayer, God is quick to intervene, and He says, 'I have to listen.' The prayer that I am talking about is called *intercession*. Let's look at 1 Timothy 2:1-4:

> [1]FIRST OF all, then, I admonish and urge that petitions, prayers, intercessions, and thanksgivings be offered on behalf of all men,

> [2]For kings and all who are in positions of authority or high responsibility, that [outwardly] we may pass a quiet and undisturbed life [and inwardly] a peaceable one in all godliness and reverence and seriousness in every way.

> [3]For such [praying] is good and right, and [it is] pleasing and acceptable to God our Saviour,

> [4]Who wishes all men to be saved and [increasingly] to perceive and recognize and discern and know precisely and correctly the [divine] Truth. (Amplified Bible)

In this passage of Scripture, it is evident that intercession pleases God. By definition, intercession is basically 'standing in the gap' on behalf of others. When you are going through a difficult time, all of your emotions are pushing you contrary to this concept—you are generally pushed towards yourself. However, I believe that God is calling us to shift our focus, especially when we are going through trying times. When a person is about only him/herself, I assure you that person will not accomplish anything great for the Kingdom of God because the kingdom is all about communities. Likewise, a church community should not focus on one or two individuals because that will not please God, and He will not draw near to that community. Let me share this absolute with you: the more you begin to focus on others, in spite of what you are going through, the more God looks after your needs, as stated in Matthew 6:33:

> [33]But seek (at and strive after) first of His entire kingdom and His righteousness ([His] way of doing and being right), and then all these things taken together will be given you besides. (Amplified Bible)

DEVELOPING A SPIRITUAL WARFARE MENTALITY IN THE
MIDDLE OF THE VALLEY

When you intercede, you send a clear message to God that He can do kingdom business with you because you are not about self. You are also making an indirect statement to Him that you can be trusted with the lives of others. Remember, Christ wishes that all men may be saved; therefore, you have an important part to play in that role.

We need to understand that our intercessory prayers create possibilities in the earth for the Spirit of God to move in great ways. When we cease to pray for others, it creates an atmosphere of hopelessness and barrenness in a community. What is there to hope for? Intercession gives you something to hope for in life. Similarly, it also gives God a channel through which to work; that is why He is constantly seeking intercessors:

> And I sought a man among them who should build up the wall and stand in the gap before Me for the land that I should not destroy it, but I found none. (Ezek. 22:30; Amplified Bible)

When you stand as an intercessor, you also become a voice that God can use to send and release hope in the lives of people. It is unfortunate that a lot of people are suffering from the dreadful disease of hopelessness and despair. However, as bad as it may be, you have been designated by God to be that beacon of hope to a hopeless world, which is crying out for purpose and significance in life. I believe that God wants to challenge us to think differently. Begin to intercede for the people that God has 'put on' your heart and don't give up. Your perseverance in intercessory prayer has the power to cancel out divorces, suicides, sicknesses and diseases, hopelessness, and any other things that are not in line with God's original plan for mankind.

Paul and Silas Got It!

Let us examine this brief account of an event in the life of Paul and Silas and extract some powerful principles that can affect our mentalities:

> [25]About midnight Paul and Silas were praying and singing hymns to God, and the other prisoners were listening to them. [26]Suddenly there was such a violent earthquake that the foundations of the prison were shaken. At once all the prison doors flew open, and everyone's chains came loose. [27]The jailer woke up, and when he saw the prison doors

open, he drew his sword and was about to kill himself because he thought the prisoners had escaped. [28]But Paul shouted, 'Don't harm yourself! We are all here!'

[29]The jailer called for lights, rushed in and fell trembling before Paul and Silas. [30]He then brought them out and asked, 'Sirs, what must I do to be saved?' (Acts 16:25-29; NIV)

This situation occurred just after Paul had cast an evil spirit out of a woman. Paul and Silas were beaten and thrown into prison because they had affected somebody's fortune-telling occupation. One of the most important principles that we can extract from this account is the men's response to adversity. They got to a point, where they forgot about their circumstances and they began to pray and sing unto the Lord. I believe God intervened very powerfully because the men had got the revelation about prayer: 'What you are going through is not about you.' Knowing who Paul was, I don't believe that he spent the entire time saying, 'God only get me and Silas out of here, and save us.'

It is my belief that he spent time calling forth the will of God in the midst of the situation and interceding for the other men as well. That caught the attention of God so much that He could not help but to intervene and bring forth His purpose in their midst. This intervention had a domino effect because the jailer and his household were eventually saved through spiritual conversion and baptism.

Lessons to be Learnt!

Do not underestimate the purpose of your trials and the power of your intercession. It is prayer that gets results, as seen in the life of Paul and Silas. Another important principle to learn is that you should never see people as your real enemy; otherwise, you will have difficulty interceding on their behalf. Learn to see the purpose of God in them and pray that into existence, then God will move on their behalf and save them. I guess that is one of the reasons that Jesus has also instructed us to forgive people who have wronged us. When you don't forgive them, it will be impossible for you to pray forth the purposes of God in their lives. For this reason, we ought to walk in forgiveness at all times, or we will not be able walk fully in our purpose.

It is amazing that God can elevate your perceived enemies and use them for the glory of His kingdom. When we begin to love people, we will want to see them come to a place of purpose. This is a serious place of maturity to which God is calling us. I believe that God's grace is also available to help us in this area if we are willing to let Him rule.

Praying in the Spirit!

Let us examine a few principles about praying in the spirit. I find that praying in the spirit can be particularly useful, especially when we don't know what to say. A lot of times we find ourselves in situations where we are not sure what to say; therefore, the best thing to do is to get the first response from God's perspective. This is a unique experience in that it enables you to tap into a supernatural realm of hope and possibilities. The Scripture says that praying in other tongues will edify you (1 Cor. 14:4). The word 'edify' means 'to build up' or 'to restore'. Sometimes when we are facing hardships, we tend to become broken in spirit. When we pray in an unknown tongue, God restores our soul.

The word 'restore' means 'to return back'. Through the work and power of His Spirit, God does not allow us to return to the place, where we used to be, maybe one or two years before. He restores us to the original place that He, before the foundations of the earth, had destined for us to be. This is 'restoration' because where you used to be is not good enough for where God wants you to be. What we need to understand is that our spirit is perfect. It is the soul that continuously needs to be redeemed and lined up with the Word of God. Accordingly, when we pray in the spirit, God begins to build up our minds, will, and intellects (emotions), and He shows us how to line up these components of our lives with His Word. Remember that the Holy Spirit is not a dictator; He leads us into all truth. When you pray in an unknown tongue, you are basically giving the Holy Spirit permission to restore your soul by showing you how to refashion your mind, will, and emotions in accordance with God's divine principles.

Praying in tongues also builds up your faith (Jude 20). When you are engaged in doing this, you do not know what you are saying. You are totally speaking by faith. If you do not believe in the unknown tongue, then it will not work for you. However, if you do believe, then it will work for you because it is proof that you believe in the power of the Holy Spirit, in spite of what is happening around you. When you pray in the spirit, you are essentially saying, *'Lord, I believe in You. I don't know what is happening around me, but I put my confidence in You. I believe that You will lead me into all truth because You are my guiding comforter and I trust your Holy Spirit.'* It takes faith to do this!

What would you rather have than God's perfect will? Praying in tongues helps us to pray God's perfect will, even when we are clueless about what we are saying (Rom. 8:26). Jesus said that His food is to do the will of God. That's an emphatic statement! Praying in an unknown tongue exposes us to the perfect will of God, which is a place that our hearts should long to be. We need the will of God in our workplace, marriage, community, family, business, ministry, nation, etc. Let us consistently tap into this realm of prayer as we expose and sensitise ourselves to God's perfect will. What are you waiting for?

CHAPTER 10

The Deadly Weapons of Praise: Understanding the Psychology of Praise

IT IS FUNNY how life can be defined by key moments. As Jesus was riding His donkey through Jerusalem, people were chanting His praises and some were even ready to enthrone Him as their king for they echoed, 'King of the Jews.' It's remarkable that many people were singing His praises at that point in time. If the life story of Jesus had ended then, you would probably have thought, 'Boy, those people really loved to praise God.' On the contrary, some of those said people, in the presence of Pilate, at another moment were chanting, 'Crucify Him!' It's amazing how life can be very enigmatic. One day, something entices us, and in the twinkling of another moment, something causes our interest to be diverted. Is this really human nature? Do we have to become like this?

If you don't know by now, I am a very curious character. I consider myself a 'want-to-know' person. What can cause a person in one moment to praise God and in another moment chant along with everybody else, 'Crucify Him!?' I don't know about you, but I am curious to find the answer because many have fallen victim to that mentality. In addition, my objective is to strengthen you so that you are able to press forward at all times and do not become like the people who fell victim to peer pressure and chanted the crucifixion of our Lord.

This term 'The Psychology of Praise' focuses on an interesting concept that I have formulated. Remember, warfare is all about territory! Whoever says that spiritual warfare is not about territory does not understand the heart of God. Why do you think God created the earth? God is obsessed with territory because He is a king and all kings love territories. Let me make my first important statement about praise: praising God is as important to you as it is to God. I am sure that you have heard statements, such as 'every relationship is built on trust' or 'the strength of a relationship is built on trust'.

In a previous chapter, I spoke about the importance of trusting God. However, I want to highlight a very important principle, which is that praising God has psychological advantages that will propel you forward in warfare. Psychology is the study of mind and behaviour; therefore, it is easy to conclude that your mind is the most powerful asset that you have. As a parent, you would literally spend thousands of dollars (at minimum) on your children's education.

You would make all these investments in hope of stimulating the child's mind so that he or she may be eventually transformed into a productive citizen. Likewise, you are also looking at it as an immediate and as a long-term investment. For example, in kindergarten or infant school, you would expect to see your child counting, singing, reasoning, comprehending, etc. When your child goes to a higher grade or class, you expect to see more holistic growth in his capacity to learn and in the development of his comprehension skills. If a child eventually becomes a doctor, it is not just what he or she learnt in medical school that made the difference. It was the foundation laid from birth and built upon during pre-kindergarten, which became strengthened in kindergarten, infant, primary, secondary, and tertiary institutions. Certainly, all levels of education played a key role in the development of that person.

What's the Point!

As people of God, we need to get a revelation that praise is a learned action and its strength and vitality is developed through consistency. Anything learnt is developed through consistency. If you consider the work ethics of great athletes and musicians, you will acknowledge how disciplined and consistent they are. On the same note, you ought to praise God consistently through your speech, shouting, dancing, clapping, musical instruments, etc. Psychologically, you will be creating a distance between your short-term and long-term memory.

A problem for many people is that they have merely a short-term memory of God's unfailing nature. The more you praise God, the more you move from a short-term to a long-term (eternal) perception of His greatness and vastness. When David was tending the sheep, He spent a lot of time praising God. Psychologically, those praises recorded a fixed image of God in his mind, heart, and soul. David spent countless times setting his mind on the things that were above as he praised God; this enabled him to develop tremendous strength and courage. Why do you think that David was not afraid to approach Goliath? All those hours that he practised in praise, developed an indelible image of an unfailing God.

Moreover, when nobody wanted to fight Goliath, David was ready to kill him. He had already gone through his training and was infused with confidence and boldness. I have discovered that one of the main reasons having a fixed image of God is important is that the more we see God, the more we see ourselves. When you praise Him consistently, you see nothing but His nature within which you find yourself. Praise blocks away a great deal of negative thoughts and emotions because the focus shifts from self (circumstances) to God. Not only are you seeing a great God but also, psychologically, you discover your greatness within that context and you muster up the strength to fight any battle that comes your way. In other words, your mind becomes open, and you begin to think, *'If God is great and faithful and I am created in His image and likeness, then I am great too.'*

In life, it is merely our mentalities that make a huge difference in the way we function. As human beings, our minds can become contaminated with the filths of this world; thus, the key to advancement is developing a praiseworthy attitude towards God. Let's look at what King Jehoshaphat did:

> [21]After consulting the people, Jehoshaphat appointed men to sing to the LORD and to praise him for the splendor of his holiness as they went out at the head of the army, saying:
> 'Give thanks to the LORD, for his love endures forever.'
>
> [22]As they began to sing and praise, the LORD set ambushes against the men of Ammon and Moab and Mount Seir who were invading Judah, and they were defeated. (2 Chr. 20:21-22; NIV)

The principle that we can learn from David and Jehoshaphat, is that praise paves the way for victory. Remember, the greatest victory is in the mind. I believe that it is easy for God to work a miracle in the earth. But the challenging part is for God to work a miracle in your mind because He

STANLEY R. SAUNDERS

needs your full cooperation. Whenever your hope is down, and you don't feel particularly strong in your mind, then it's a clear indication that your praise level is running on empty! What are you going to do about that? That is not a good place to be. Allow God to programme your mind through praise so that you can see and experience the salvation of the Lord.

Let's look at this Scripture:

> ¹At that time the disciples came to Jesus and asked, 'Who, then, is the greatest in the kingdom of heaven?'
>
> ²He called a little child to him, and placed the child among them. ³And he said: 'Truly I tell you, unless you change and become like little children, you will never enter the kingdom of heaven. (Matt. 18:1-2; NIV)

If you ask a six-year-old to solve the following problem 'one plus one', he or she will respond by saying, 'two'. Once this child has grasped the concept of counting, there is absolutely nothing that you can say or do that would change the fact that 'one plus one' equals 'two' in that child's mind. It becomes a fixed reality in that child's mind whether there is a drought, or it is raining, snowing, or hailing. Similarly, if we develop a praiseworthy attitude towards God, then there is absolutely nothing—be it hard times, economic recession, sickness, wars, conflict—that would change our perception of the unchanging, loving God. As a matter fact, when, with the right attitude of praise, you, like David, face these challenges, it will radically enhance your perception of God and self.

Furthermore, this is why the Bible says:

> ¹I will bless the LORD at all times: his praise shall continually be in my mouth. ²My soul shall make her boast in the LORD: the humble shall hear thereof, and be glad. ³O magnify the LORD with me, and let us exalt his name together. ⁴I sought the LORD, and he heard me, and delivered me from all my fears. (Ps. 24:1-4; NIV)

When you have this attitude, it will create an indelible image of hope within your heart, regardless of your circumstances. I want to give you three keys that would develop a praiseworthy attitude:

Key No. 1: Verbalising

Have you ever wondered why God gave you a voice? Well, this is one of the reasons: to bring forth His praises in the earth. It's important that we continuously echo His praises from our lips. Like prayers, the more we practise and train our minds, the more customary praise becomes. Remember, practice makes perfect. Do you want a fresh perspective of God? Then begin to praise and keep praise coming from your heart, even if you do not understand why you are going through certain circumstances, continue to praise. How does faith come? Faith comes by hearing and by hearing of the Word of God.

The more you verbalise praise, it will affect your faith life. When you are constantly hearing about the greatness of God, you will grow in that belief, and it will eventually govern your mind and lifestyle. Remember, whatever you believe is a product of what you are hearing and thinking. That is why you need to train your ears to hear the Lord's praises, which will then stimulate your brain.

Key No. 2: Writing

Another important principle that you can apply, is writing. It's a really good idea to have your writing reflecting the praises of the Lord. Why? It helps you to remember the goodness of the Lord. That is why I highly recommend that people document or make journals of praise reports. Documenting your praise reports, you will have a point of reference. For example, if you are going through a difficult time, you can look through your archives, and, as you acknowledge that God had delivered you before, it will definitely help to rekindle praises from deep within you. What it also does is that it breathes a spirit of expectation. By this, I mean that you would want to add to your journal. You would want God to do more things for you because He had done it before:

> 6And I am convinced and sure of this very thing, that He Who began a good work in you will continue until the day of Jesus Christ [right up to the time of His return], developing [that good work] and perfecting and bringing it to full completion in you. (Phil. 1:6; Amplified Bible)

In concluding this point about writing, I wish to reiterate that your praises really bring what I call a 'Philippians 1:6' attitude upon you. You naturally want God to complete the work in your life. There is an assurance that what you are going through is not the end. Therefore, my praise is inviting God to complete the unfinished business that He has started in my life. This is one of my revelations: You should never stop praising God because God has no end. In other words, God is not finished! Who told you that God is finished? God will never be finished because He is God. When people cease to praise Him, they are saying in essence that 'God is finished'. That is a defeatist mentality!

Whenever I document the goodness of God, it brings a sense of hope, which I cannot vividly explain. It enhances my perception of God, and I see Him as the possibility in the midst of impossibility. That is a wonderful place to be!

Key No. 3: Conversing

Do you like to have a good conversation? I am amazed at how some people could spend hours in conversation with just one person. Sometimes I wonder if they would ever stop conversing. I have a friend who would literally spend hours talking on the phone. (You can just imagine what her phone bill would be). I believe that God created us as conversational beings so that we can ultimately have healthy relationships; however, there are some conversations that do more harm than good. The nature of your conversations is more important than with whom you are conversing.

What do you talk about? This is a very important question that you need to grasp. In the context of praise, it is very important that you always allow your conversations to reflect the praises of God. Have you ever spoken to someone who seemed to literally wear you down? What I mean is that after a conversation with such a person you feel mentally drained. Why is that? When you hear a constant flow of negative reports, it can emotionally wear you down and cause mental fatigue. Let me give you some seeds of wisdom.

Whenever you talk with someone, always try to direct the conversation to a positive or praiseworthy subject. For example, if you are talking with somebody who is extremely negative, try to let him/her see the goodness of God in the midst of his/her situation. I believe that if you do not guard your heart with all diligence, those negative, depressing vibes can be transferred to you subconsciously. Therefore, it is your responsibility to direct the flow of those conversations so that you will not only help the person through his/her trials, but you will also preserve your praiseworthy attitude at the same time. If such person refuses to see the 'light at the end of the tunnel', then limit your conversation and pray for that person. Don't try to play the role of a super hero. Remember, change is up to the individual. You cannot change anybody.

We need to be careful because if we do not guard our hearts, there are some people who would just wear us down, stifle our inflow of joy, and subsequently kill our praiseworthy attitude to the Lord. What you want to do in your conversations is to be an optimistic leader (be positive always). Let people know or see the goodness of God in your speech so that their eyes and minds may be open. You would be surprised that one simple conversation can really uplift somebody's spirit if you are open and sensitive to their needs.

With God, all things are possible if we are willing to apply these principles to our daily lives. This is one way in which we can exercise dominion in the earth! When you are positive in your conversations, it transfers hope into your home, workplace, church community, neighbourhood, etc. Ladies and gentlemen, the Kingdom of God is wholly about bringing hope to a hopeless generation; and, in doing that, we take territories in every sector of society. Are you ready to lead your conversations?

Operation Inhabitation

I will close this chapter by giving you my take on Psalm 22, which, by the way, is one of my favourite Scriptures in the Bible. The verses read:

> [3]But thou art holy, O thou that inhabitest the praises of Israel. [4]Our fathers trusted in thee: they trusted, and thou didst deliver them. [5]They cried unto thee, and were delivered: they trusted in thee, and were not confounded. (Ps. 22:3-5; KJV)

The Greek word for 'inhabit' is yâshab, which means to 'dwell, remain, sit, abide'. It is very important to keep in mind that God is not merely a king, but he is the King of kings. Whenever you are talking about where a king sits, you are talking about the place from which the king reigns. You are also talking about a place from where power, authority, favour, protection, and blessings flow. In other words, your praises speak volumes: praises invite God to reign in your midst, and where God reigns, there is power, authority, favour, protection, blessings, and prosperity. In addition, your praise is a kingdom-language and a mark of stewardship. It's a declaration that you are no longer in charge. Over what areas of your life does God need to reign? Begin to praise and allow Him to sit in that area, then you will see a tremendous difference.

God has instructed us to praise Him with instruments—the ten-string ones are included too. According to physician Alfred A. Tomatis, M. D. (1920-2001), there is a relationship between certain sound frequencies and their effect on functions of the mind and body. He discovered that certain sound frequencies affect different abilities. Dr. Tomatis categorised his research into three zones: zone one; zone two; and zone three. Zone one is 'sensory integration', which is also called 'lower frequency sounds'. This affects your balance, rhythm, coordination, etc.

After that, there is zone two 'speech and language', which affects your memory, concentration, attention, speech, language, and vocal control. Then there is zone three 'high spectrum', which is called 'higher frequency sounds'. This is believed to affect your energy, intuition, ideals, ideas, spirituality, and creativity. I humbly believe that this study is showing how God designed praise to work for us.

The greater our praise frequency is, the more effect it will have on us. God dwells where there are sounds of praises by invading our minds, concentration, and speech. A lot of physicians use music to develop these areas. This is really beyond human understanding! I have been in environments, where people who came in and created a disgusting atmosphere by their cursing, which had so much of a negative effect on the surroundings that it literally stifled productivity in the work/home environments. On the contrary, I have been in environments, where there were sounds of praises, and there was a peaceful and productive atmosphere in the home/work environments. I am not suggesting that you should strike up a band in your workplace, but, with your praise, you can change the atmosphere. Each and every one of us has the potential to change our environment with our speech or song. When our speech and song are in correlation with our praiseworthy attitude and reflect the goodness of God, the outcome will be the creation of contagious, awe-inspiring atmospheres.

The great physician also designed the sound of praise to affect certain areas of our lives by bringing a great level of focus on our minds. Moreover, as the sound frequency increases, it has the potential to affect our energies, intuitions, ideals, ideas, spirituality, and creativity. I notice that many times, in the midst of my praising, I feel energised. Believe me when I say that it is during this time that God births a lot of creative ideas through you. This is the type of effect that praise has on you! It opens up your mind to the limitless creativity of God.

On a practical note, the more creativity and innovativeness we apply, the more valuable we become to our communities and the Kingdom of God. Therefore, if we can tap into this realm, there is no limit to where God can take us. The men who invented 'Facebook' have been able to put their mark on a large territory. I believe that, in the same way, God is calling His people to arise and take territories for Him in the areas, such as technology, tourism, politics, business, and education. As people of God, we have no reasons not to be used by God. Are you using your weapon of praise? Are you focused, creative, energetic, intuitive, and joyful? Are you constantly flowing with new ideas? What is your excuse again?

CHAPTER 11

The Weapon of Truth as the Sword of Freedom

CAN YOU HANDLE the truth? Truth is really an interesting concept because everybody has his/her own reaction to it. Do you know of a person who does not like to be corrected? What do you really think about that person? I am sure that you do not have a positive outlook of that person. Why? It is easy to tell the destiny of a person who does not embrace the truth, right? Unfortunately, we live in a world, where people have been forming their own principles to suit themselves and distinguish them from others. I guess that by nature, mankind likes to have things done in their own ways because it is more of a pleasurable convenience. Is there anything wrong with that?

> [12]There is a way which seems right to a man and appears straight before him, but at the end of it is the way of death. (Prov. 14:12; Amplified Bible)

From what the Bible tells, you know that if you don't embrace the truth of the kingdom, the outcome will be death. In this context 'death' is not limited to a literal or physical thing because you can be alive but not functional. Jesus said:

> [31]To the Jews who had believed him, Jesus said, 'If you hold to my teaching, you are really my disciples. [32]Then you will know the truth, and the truth will set you free.' (John 8:31-32; NIV)

One of the first points I want to make is that truth is designed to free you from a malfunctioned state to a functional state. It is beyond the fact that you are no longer living in sin. The more you hold on to the teaching of the kingdom, the more significant you become to your world. Freedom comes with responsibility! Now that God has freed you from sin, you are responsible to hold on to His truth for your dear life. God desires an abundant life for each of us, so we need to love the truth if we want to walk into our destiny.

'Your attitude towards the truth hidden in God's word is a photograph of your maturity and prosperity.'

I want you to understand that your attitude towards the truth is a threefold revelation, encompassing your past, present and future. Let's examine the concept of the past. I once heard somebody saying, 'You are not free until your past has no effect on your future.' That's a profound statement! You may have made some mistakes yesterday, but yesterday is gone. Perhaps you may have accomplished some great things, but yesterday has gone like the wind. It is true that yesterday has moved on from us, but it is weird that sometimes we are still longing to be with her. Do you know that yesterday does not care about you? Why? Yesterday is busy having an affair with your past. They have a serious love affair, and there is nothing that you can do to get between them. I have some advice for you! Why not leave them alone and let them be. There is somebody else out there that is better for you. Do you want me to introduce you to her?

Present

I would like to introduce you to my friend 'Now'. You can also refer to her as 'Today' or 'Present'. If you treat her well, she will always be with you. If you mistreat her, then you will live in regret because there is no turning back. The question that I have for you is: Are you willing to accommodate her? Is there any room for the truth in your life? King Herod wanted to kill truth. The Pharisees also wanted to kill the truth (John, Chapter 8). Why do so many people want to kill the truth? Well, because once you embrace her, she will completely change your life. She will take over every area of your life so much that the world will not even recognise you. The longer you become married to her, the more you will become like her. She will have you doing things that you never thought you could do. By the way, once you embrace, you do not have to be concerned about your future because she will become everything that you will ever need.

STANLEY R. SAUNDERS

Mirror! Mirror!

Do you have a mirror at home? People place mirrors in their homes so that they can have a clear and honest view of themselves, especially before going somewhere. Most people like to know how they look. It's just human nature! In general, people get excited when you compliment them on their appearance. As a matter of fact, if a single man keeps on complimenting a woman on her appearance, he might eventually get her to be his spouse. On the contrary, why do we tend to put up resistance when someone gives us quite the opposite of a compliment?

What if your teacher tells you that you need to work harder? What if your pastor or your superior at work tells you that you need to be more committed? What if your wife says you are not spending enough time with her? Why have you been so frustrated and angry lately? What are you afraid of? These are just some of the questions that confront people on a daily basis. If we are to move forward in life, we first have to come to grips with the truth and learn from it. I have a simple theory: 'If you don't learn from the truth you will never learn.' Life is not as difficult as we tend to make it. If we embrace the truth of God's Word, then that would eliminate many of the problems that we face.

'The Truth Serves as an Anti-Virus Against Deception'

The bottom line is this: God wants you to function so that you can accomplish His work and serve His purpose on all the earth. Please bear in mind that God speaks through leaders, parents, teachers, spouses, dreams, visions, children, His written Word, His audible voice, thoughts, etc. Truth preserves purpose. If you are open to it, it will take you on a long prosperous journey. God has placed people in your life for a reason and a season. I have discovered that a person can learn a lot about him/herself from others. What makes you upset? What drives you absolutely insane? Oftentimes, you learn the truth from your interaction with others. If you are a married man and you want to know the truth about yourself, ask your wife. I am certain that she will reveal it to you even if you don't ask her.

Once you embrace the truth of God's Word, there will be no room for deception in your life. It's like having a container of water. Once the container of water is full, then there is no space for anything else. Likewise, this is the approach that we need to take in our spiritual journey. We need to fill ourselves so much with the truth that there is no ground for the enemy to work. The number one tactic of the enemy is to fight through deception so that you begin to doubt your purpose and subsequently second-guess God. When you begin to doubt God, especially in challenging times, it affects the way you relate to Him, which directly affects your level of faith.

During Job's hardships, the enemy was trying to convince him to curse God and die. In other words, he was telling Job: 'Your God has failed you. Take a look at what you are going through. You will never overcome this problem.' Whenever you believe the lie of the enemy, it's a clear indication that deception has knocked at your door and invited himself for dinner. That is trouble because he does not like to leave without a fight, and the longer he remains in your home, the more comfortable he becomes; it will be only a matter of time before he takes over your house. If he is in your house, you need to serve him an eviction notice, and, if he is not in your house, don't even think about entertaining him.

The reason you have to buckle yourself with the truth is that truth holds everything together. It holds your faith, righteousness, hope, words, and actions together. When you buckle your pants with a belt, you are preventing your body from being exposed because the pants cover you from being vulnerable to others. That is similar to the power of the truth if you buckle yourself with it. It takes away your vulnerability and enhances your usability. In John, Chapter 8, Jesus was telling the Pharisees that He could not use them in His kingdom because they did not love the truth:

> [44]You are of your father, the devil, and it is your will to practice the lusts and gratify the desires [which are characteristic] of your father. He was a murderer from the beginning and does not stand in the truth, because there is no truth in him. When he speaks a falsehood, he speaks what is natural to him, for he is a liar [himself] and the father of lies and of all that is false.

> [45]But because I speak the truth, you do not believe Me [do not trust Me, do not rely on Me, or adhere to Me]. (John 8:44-45 Amplified Bible)

How profound is that statement! If you do not love the truth, then you are no different from the murderers and the liars, and your father is the devil. That's a coarse but accurate statement! If you reject His Word then you are not of God, and you will die because Jesus said, 'If a man keeps my saying,

STANLEY R. SAUNDERS

he shall never taste of death.' Truth brings purpose and meaning to life. Human beings are on a quest to find truth because they want significance to their lives.

What is the Purpose of Truth?

The purpose of truth is to deliver man's soul from a religiously decomposed state to a functional and productive position in God's kingdom. It is clear that God wants you free so that you can accomplish greater kingdom work. Let us allow God to invade our minds with His truth and walk in victory. Our future in God is very bright if we hold on to His truth, which cannot fail. God cannot fail us; He has great things in store for those who love His Word and are willing to walk according to His statutes.

CHAPTER 12

The Weapons of Salvation— Thinking and the Preparation of the Gospel of Peace

I MAGINE THAT YOU have won an all-expense paid vacation to anywhere in the world. The free package includes first-class tickets, luxury suites, tour relaxation treatment, food, shopping spree, and anything else you can imagine. I am certain that you would take advantage of this once-in-a-lifetime offer, right?

Question?

Can you say that you have fully enjoyed yourself if you remained confined to your hotel room for the entire vacation period? You mean you actually went on a vacation and did not take advantage of the free tour? How about the relaxation treatments and the shopping spree? I can't believe that you did not take advantage of those; after all, they were free. In reference to God's kingdom, it is clear that salvation is one of the prerequisites to inherit such a paradise (His kingdom). What I want you to understand is that the free vacation package represents the free gift of salvation.

Many people are of the belief that the concept of salvation lends itself merely to being born again. When a person becomes born again, it is good to rejoice because the soul will not perish eternally. However, after saying the 'sinner's prayer', the person has to live on earth and be a productive kingdom-citizen. One of the definitions of salvation is 'deliverance from sin and its consequences'. Another definition of salvation is 'preservation from harm, ruins or loss'. I am sure that as you look around you see people affected by sicknesses, diseases, debts, losses, fear, terrorism, uncertainties, and every other imaginable adversity. The essence of salvation is also in the aftermath of the sinner's prayer. Now that I am born again and saved because of the shed blood of Jesus, what's next? The answer to that is also the power of salvation:

> Beloved, I pray that you may prosper in every way and [that your body] may keep well, even as [I know] your soul keeps well and prospers.

> [3]In fact, I greatly rejoiced when [some of] the brethren from time to time arrived and spoke [so highly] of the sincerity and fidelity of your life, as indeed you do live in the Truth [the whole Gospel presents]. (3 John 1:2-3; Amplified)

> Why do we put God in a Box?

I am sure you know that the only way you can test your faith is through a trial. The Scripture above clearly states God's earnest desire for mankind. Salvation is about the complete deliverance from adversities in your soul, body, mind, finance, relationships, business, and every other area of your life. Stop putting God in a box! You have to start thinking 'salvation' in every situation that life presents, regardless of how you may feel. When you think 'salvation' at all times, it produces ongoing hope. Therefore, the more you fix your eyes on the author of salvation, the more hopeful you become.

This is important because we live in an era that is filled with bad news about the economy, health, politics, crime, terrorism, etc. Hence it is imperative that you remain hopeful if you want to succeed in the earth. When you think about salvation, it keeps up your countenance, and there is no room for depression and darkness in your life. Let's consider the life of King David. He constantly had to remind himself that the Lord was his salvation, especially when he was going through some of the defining moments of his life. It is comforting to note that God always delivered him because he kept thinking 'salvation' even when he was standing in front of Goliath or hiding in a cave. His salvation-thinking was his surety.

What God Cannot Do for You?

Think about this! Even though God is all-powerful, He cannot believe for you, He cannot think for you or hope for you. The onus is on you to think for yourself. Consequently, it is imperative that you set your mind on the right thing (hope of salvation). I remember when I was going through a very frustrating time at work. I called some of my dearest friends for comfort and even though they were very encouraging, I had to take control of my own emotions and endeavour to experience the salvation of the Lord. I had to take dominion over my ill feelings, discontent and bitterness, and open my eyes to the hope of the Lord.

There is salvation for you in whatever situation you might be facing. The deliverance of the Lord is on its way. If you remember when David was facing Goliath, he said:

> You come to me with a sword, a spear, and a javelin, but I come to you in the name of the Lord of hosts, the God of the ranks of Israel, Whom you have defied.

> [46]This day the Lord will deliver you into my hand and I will smite you and cut off your head. And I will give the corpses of the army of the Philistines this day to the birds of the air and the wild beasts of the earth, that all the earth may know that there is a God in Israel. [47]And all this assembly shall know that the Lord saves not with sword and spear; for the battle is the Lord's, and He will give you into our hands. (1 Sam. 17:45-47)

It does not matter how tall the mountain seems or how low the valley may appear because the salvation of the Lord is undeterred, if you believe in God. As you recount the life of David, you become aware of how much he believed and experienced the deliverance of the Lord. What are you facing? Whom are you facing? Of what are you afraid? Let me declare that there is nothing that you cannot overcome: be it sickness, depression, unemployment, recession, sin, or whatever you are facing. God has a plan for your life, and you will overcome. What you are facing is temporary! It's not the end; God will deliver you. Keep on hoping and consider it done!

Thinking Outside Yourself!

Thinking 'salvation' can also affect the lives of others. For example, there is a reason that God has put certain people (be it in your school, workplace, neighbourhood, business, church, community, etc.) in your path. You are responsible to impact the lives of these people, regardless of the circumstances that you are facing. It's like back to Eden all over again! God has put you in a garden (your workplace, family, neighbourhood, etc.) and has also given you His presence. However, He is demanding that you multiply, considering that He has given you all the resources you need to accomplish that process. In short, with the hope that God has given you, you must help others to arrive at a place of deliverance and freedom.

Let me mention that you would never be satisfied until you arrive at a place of impact. The reason we are frustrated at times is that we have not reached our optimum level of kingdom-impact, and God has designed us to release that continually into our world. Often, people would say, 'Something is missing.' To me, the answer to that is simple: Find somebody to impact within your world and that will bring a great level of satisfaction in your life. We need to stop feeling sorry for ourselves and begin to impact the lives of people around us. God has strategically placed, along your path, people who are waiting for a word from you, who have the God-given resources to help bring freedom to their lives. What are you waiting on? What is your excuse?

The Preparation of the Gospel of Peace

This is an interesting concept, for most people have merely a religious understanding of the Gospel. Myles Munroe often stated that we ought to preach the gospel of the kingdom and not the gospel of Jesus. I am certain that most religious folks hearing such a statement would scratch their heads. However, I think that we have to be real with people and let them understand who they are and what they possess on the inside. In my humble opinion, the preparation of the Gospel of Peace is very simple. As people of God's Kingdom, we are vessels of solution. We have solutions trapped on the inside of us. For every difficulty that we are facing, God has a solution within us to overcome it because we have the Word of God stored deep within us.

The more you store the principles of God's Word within you, the more competent you can become to solve whatever problems you are facing in your family, marriage, community, government, etc. When you input the Word of God, you are actually storing potential solutions. Let's look at it this way: The Word of God is full of potentials that can solve every conceivable problem on this earth. However, even though this is a fact, it does not guarantee that it will work for all of us. The word 'preparation' is the power in this statement. When you do things haphazardly and you call it 'in the spirit', you get poor results, and often you end up worse off than the way you had started.

The Power of Preparation

By definition, 'preparation' is 'the work or planning involved in making something or somebody ready, or in putting something together in advance' (Encarta Dictionary). We do not want to be like the foolish virgins who were not prepared to meet their bride. Please note that you are not guaranteed second and third chances in life; this is why it is imperative that you constantly prepare yourself to be a solution in whatever environment God has placed you.

How Can You Prepare Yourself to be a Solution?

One of the first things that I like to tell people is: 'be diligent in your environment.' Diligence is a principle that gives you a voice in the midst of difficulties. For example, we need to understand that nobody will listen to a rebellious and ignorant person. When you exhibit good work ethics, you automatically become a voice. Whether you like it or not, people are looking at you, and they are constantly evaluating you to see what you are worth. Employers conduct appraisals because they want to see what their employees are worth. If you have been found to be worthless, they may quickly dismiss you, without any reservations.

When you constantly upgrade yourself in knowledge, good attitude, understanding, integrity, and wisdom, you become valuable to your family, school, workplace, and community. As a result, in the midst of a crisis, people will look to you for the solution to the problem. If there is a problem in your environment and people are not coming to you for solution, then you really need to sit down and evaluate yourself. What is it that I need to change? What is wrong with my attitude? If we want to make an impact in society, it is important that we evaluate ourselves and begin to make practical changes. A lot of times we face problems in our environments because we don't have the right attitudes. We need to be like Joseph! With the ticket of diligence, Joseph prepared himself while he was in prison to be the solution to Pharaohs' problem. When it was his turn to speak, he had solutions to the problems that Egypt was facing. That is inspiring!

We need to learn to take a practical approach to life and become problem solvers. When a problem is solved, it brings an optimum level of peace to the environment and the problem solver becomes a valuable asset to the community. I want you to consider the following question. When people see you, do they see a problem solver or a problem? Take some time to think about this question as God continues to work in your heart so that you can continue to build His kingdom and leave a lasting legacy in the earth.

CHAPTER 13

The Weapon of Righteousness

JOHN RECENTLY GOT saved and thought that once he was a Christian, it guaranteed automatic success in life. To add to that, he spent years holding on to this concept because he was taught that once a person is a good Christian and does not harm anybody, he/she would experience great blessings in his/her life. One day he was in deep meditation and began to observe the world; he made some interesting discoveries. It came to his attention that many Christians were sick, penniless, tired, frustrated, unhappy, and envious of others. Initially, he thought that God was unfair because He should not allow His people to suffer to such great measures. 'Why are the wicked prevailing?' he questioned.

'What's up with you, God? He asked. Then he pondered, 'I thought that the wealth of the wicked was laid up for the righteous.' He was encouraged by a pastor to declare the statement 'The wealth of the wicked is laid up for the righteous' over his life. Guess what happened to him after months of declaring that statement. *Nothing!* So he went before God with rage and bitterness, and he began to question Him, for he felt that God had let him down by not meeting his expectations (not coming through in the way he had thought). 'Speak the Word, brother,' said another elderly man who was trying to comfort John as he was trying to sort out life.

Lesson to be Learnt!

The character John represents a great number of people who do not understand the concept 'righteousness', which really has nothing to do with religion. What I mean is that it has nothing do with how good a Christian you are or how many years you have been walking in the path of the Lord. If so many born-again believers are not experiencing the fullness of God's salvation, then there must be something wrong. I know that the devil is busy, but the Lord said in Luke 10:19:

I have given you authority to trample on snakes and scorpions and to overcome all the power of the enemy; nothing will harm you. So, if that is true, then what is our problem? Why are we so limited?

Understanding the Nature and Impact of Disobedience

If I say the word 'obedience', the first person you might think about is Jesus or maybe even Abraham because of the lifestyles—recounted in the Scriptures—that they both portrayed. Jesus lived a lifestyle of obedience while He was on the earth. Think about this: not once did he disobey his father, and it was obvious that He faced many challenges during His lifetime. Similarly, Abraham was willing to obey God after God had given him a command to sacrifice his only begotten son. On the contrary, if I say the word 'disobedience', you might say Satan, Adam, or King Saul. Why? It's clear that their lifestyles represent a pattern of disobedience, which was not pleasing unto the Lord.

One of the first things that we need to understand about God is that He hates disobedience with a passion. He hates this attribute because it stifles kingdom advancement and creates an atmosphere of barrenness. Every act of disobedience comes from a pattern of wrong thinking. Therefore, it is important to understand that wrong-thinking patterns create disobedient acts. Righteousness is all about developing and walking in the right character. What makes a movie great is each person's portrayal of a specific character, in accordance with the storyline and the theme. You could be acting a scene and do some dynamic stunts, but if it's not in line with the storyline and theme, the director would say, 'Cut!' I find it amazing that the word 'righteousness' simply means 'obedience'. In Ephesians, Chapter 6, God gives us a very simple instruction, which is to put on righteousness. One of the interesting things about a Roman soldier is that his breastplate is visible. It is always visible to his enemy, and so indicates that the enemy cannot penetrate that area because it is sealed. Righteousness is a visible trait that you cannot hide because it shines like the sun even in the midst of darkness.

Knowing that I am a minister of the gospel, people are always asking me for a 'word'. They like to say, 'Give me a 'word', brother'. Or they ask, 'What is the Lord saying?' It seems like people always want a fresh 'word'. My new response to people is 'Put on obedience: obey your leaders, obey your parents, and all those who are in authority.' Whenever I tell people this, they usually give me a strange body language as if it is not what they wanted to hear. Most of the times people want to hear either: 'the Lord will bless you with great wealth', or 'you will be a great leader'. The Bible clearly states that *'To obey is better than sacrifice . . . ' (1 Sam. 15:22).* What God is saying here is that your character is greater than what you are trying to achieve because what you are working towards is subject to change, but the character is eternal. It is the part of you that touches God because it says, 'I want to be used by the Lord, regardless of the price I have to pay.'

Most, if not all of you, will agree with me that we often make sacrifices half-heartedly because we somehow feel that God will disrupt our lives. Why do we, at times, feel like God is this strange figure who goes around merely subtracting things from His children? From where does this mind-set come? Who told you that? God is not interested in your possession; He is interested in your heart's position. In fact, if you understand what Kingdom represents, you would know then that everything on the earth is the Lord's and that you are merely a steward.

I strongly sense that God has been wrestling with some of you. He has been telling you to let go of certain mindsets, attitudes, habits, struggles, and offences. Perhaps, He might be telling you to forgive someone who might have hurt you in the past. It's sad that a lot of people are ministering with heavy hearts because of offence and strife, but God is still calling them to let go of those hurts. This is one of the most challenging things that we will have to work out. I know that there are some people who may have been hurt by parents, teachers, siblings, co-workers, supervisors, pastors, spouses, neighbours, or even their friends. Maybe you genuinely want to move forward, but you find it challenging because of the hurt that you are experiencing. I want to challenge you, in accordance with God's Word, to release your emotional hurt and pain.

Hurt Destroys Purpose!

> And forgive us our sins, for we ourselves also forgive everyone who is indebted to us [who has offended us or done us wrong]. And bring us not into temptation but rescue us from evil. (Luke 11:4; Amp)

I urge you to not forget that Jesus included forgiveness when He was teaching His disciples how to pray. In Verse 2 of the above-mentioned chapter, He talks about God's kingdom, which is the most important aspect and purpose of prayer. However, in Verse 4, He talks about forgiveness and temptations that can destroy kingdom-advancement. God cannot reign where there is bitterness and strife. That is why a barrier was created when man sinned. Let's look at the root word for 'forgiveness'. The word 'forgive' comes from the Hebrew word 'aphie☐mi', which means 'to send forth'. When you are bitter and offended, there is no forward movement because the attention is on the hurt rather than God's purpose. When you forgive someone, you are sending the hurt forth. You are sending the hurt and the disappointment away from you so that you can walk into your destiny. Sending them forth is not a defeat for you; it's all about God's purpose for your life, which should be your priority. When God's purpose becomes your priority, you will forgive quickly because you will not want anything to hinder that movement. Therefore, as people of God, we need to evaluate our lives and do some sending-forth to make room for God's kingdom. Forgiveness brings peace that surpasses all understanding in our environments. Why do you think that the enemy tries to divide God's people with strife and bitterness? If he can successfully bring seeds of offence, then he will divide the people of God and cancel or delay the purpose of God. We have to be more vigilant and do not allow seeds of offence to grow in our environments!

Obedience is Not Convenient

Maybe you are in a backslidden state and have not spoken to God in years. I believe that God is now calling you to come and surrender your life to Him. I believe that now is the time to for us to turn our hearts to God. If you do not obey Him, then you create a distance in your relationship with Him. It's time to stop running from God and live wholeheartedly for Him. It does not matter what you might have done in the past; the fact that God is calling warrants an obedient response.

Obedience may not be always convenient for you because oftentimes God pushes us out of our comfort zone in order to demonstrate His glory. I can imagine how nonsensical it seemed when God told Noah to build an ark. 'What is an ark?' He might have questioned. One of the things that I have learnt over the years is that obedience does not require understanding; it just requires movement towards God. You need to know that you will never understand everything in life. Remember that God told Lot and his family not to look backward just go forward, but his wife disobeyed the command. Focussing on that event, we can assume that his wife might have thought, 'Why not look back? This does not make any sense.' I guess she could not rationalise why no one should look backward. When God tells you to do something, just do it! God will tell you what He needs to tell you at the appropriate time. Obedience is actually what shapes you into the perfect image of Christ. The more obedient you are, the more He can use you to expand His kingdom.

There is no Such Thing as Partial Obedience!

What if God is telling you to start that business or to prepare yourself for a promotion? What if He is telling you to write that book, reach out to a neighbour, or make a particular financial investment? What if He has given you an idea to create a unique product or service? What will you do about that? Maybe you might be a good prayer warrior, but if God has impressed certain things on your heart, you still need to obey Him. Perhaps, you might be wondering from where the money will come to start the business, but that is not an excuse to let that vision die.

Quitting is Disobedience!

Giving up on your dreams is also disobedience. Why? If you were created to become a medical doctor, then there would be a lot of patients who are dependent upon your knowledge and care. Unfortunately, if you do not become that doctor, many who can be cured by your hands will die. Likewise, if you are called to become a pastor or an evangelist, and you do not take up that vocation, then a great deal of souls will perish because of your disobedience. Whatever is your calling: to be a lawyer, doctor, politician, entrepreneur, a scientist, to name a few, you are not authorised to give up, regardless of what you are facing. The expansion of God's kingdom is dependent on stepping into your calling. Don't give up on your dreams because there is purpose attached to your dreams, and you will not be satisfied until you first fulfil your God-ordained purpose. One of the things you have to learn to do is to battle with principles, for it will help to establish you in the realms of the earth. Let's look at God's description of a 'righteous man', which will enable us to learn some great biblical principles.

Who is a Righteous man?

[8]But Noah found grace (favor) in the eyes of the Lord.

[9]This is the history of the generations of Noah. Noah was a just and righteous man, blameless in his [evil] generation; Noah walked [in habitual fellowship] with God. (Gen. 6:9-9; Amp)

We need to understand why God describes Noah as a 'righteous man', so that we can extract some of these principles and live a more productive lifestyle. One of the first things that this passage of Scripture says is that Noah found favour in the eyes of the Lord. The word 'favour' means 'pleasant'. In other words, God saw a heart that was not only available but also usable for His kingdom. God was conducting His HQE (Heart Quality Examinations) or the HQD (Heart Quality Diagnosis) throughout the earth and found only one positive result, which was Noah's heart. Noah passed the test because he possessed some outstanding qualities.

Noah was a just and righteous man; he was blameless, and he walked with God. Those were the inbuilt qualities that made him eligible to be used by God. It had nothing to do with religion or his appearance; it was all about his heart. Let's examine the term 'righteousness', which means 'lawfulness' in this context. When God saw Noah, He was staring at the heart of lawfulness. Noah was a man whose lifestyle was governed by the laws of God. Let me give you two definitions of a righteous person: (1) a righteous person is one whose character is shaped by the laws of God and (2) a person who is acting in line with the laws, principles, and standard within a God-assigned environment.

In the realms of a kingdom, whatever a king says is the law. Therefore, whatever is written in God's Words is the law, and we must obey if we are to walk in righteousness. We must condition our hearts to say 'yes' to the commands of the Lord if we desire to please Him. Saying 'yes' is the hallmark of a righteous man. From Genesis to Revelation, the Bible is filled with instructions. If we want to live an abundant life, then we must follow those instructions. Sometimes we look at the progress/successes of other people, and we wonder why they are prospering so much. It's all about laws! Sometimes we are struggling financially because we are violating the principle of financial management, such as neither tithing and giving nor saving. In this case, we are behaving very unrighteously with our finance, yet we expect God to bless us. Being righteous, in this sense, would be to give your tithes and offering, save/budget your money and make timely and wise investments.

We need to understand that God is no respecter of person. If you behave unrighteously in any area of your life, you will reap corruption. We need to align ourselves continuously with the principles for various areas of our lives, such as our physical bodies, minds, emotions, and financial affairs. You can be a saved person bound for heaven, but you are living like a 'pauper' in the earth because of your unrighteous practices. Whether you like it or not, this earth revolves around laws, and in order for you to survive, you must live according to the corresponding laws.

Righteousness Goes Way beyond the Scope of Christianity!

The laws of righteousness can work for you whether you are a Christian or not. I know of an anointed prophetess who was working for a private company. I am telling you that this lady could hear in the spirit like none other. However, the problem with this prophetess was that instead of doing what she was hired to do, she was giving prophetic words. She was eventually fired by her supervisor and replaced with an ungodly woman. The bottom line is that there are laws and policies of the workplace, and if you violate those laws, you will face the consequences, whether you are saved and highly anointed or you are not saved. In fact, God expects you to obey those who are in authority so that you are in right standing with them. That's the power of the gospel. T. D Jakes likes to say, 'If you work the Word, the Word will work for you.' In the case of the prophetess, she did not work the Word, so the Word did not work for her.

Three Keys to Developing Righteousness

Key No. 1: Study the Laws

If you are working for an organisation, one of the first things that you would want to do is to familiarise yourself with its policies. Why? Following policies and guidelines will determine how long you will remain with that organisation. If you do not follow the organisational standards, you will not function accurately and will stifle the goals and objectives. I think that one of the reasons God wants us to obey people in authority is that He is a God of order, authority, and structure. As a kingdom person, you cannot influence an environment if you are not in it. Therefore, when you submit to authority, you become a voice and an influence. However, we need to be wise like David and study the laws and hide them in our hearts, or be like Joshua and meditate on the laws day and night. The more you study the laws, the less likely you are to violate them. David mentions that he hid God's laws in his heart so that he would not sin against God. We need to arrive at a place, whereby we desire the laws of God above everything else.

Key No. 2: Seek Comprehension of the Laws

'Comprehension' is when you grasp the meaning of something. This is an important part of life because when you fully understand something, you will be able to make proper application. Understanding God's laws will help you to understand the heart of God. A new law regarding ammunition was passed in Belize. In a nutshell, if an unlicensed firearm is found in a home, then everybody in the home could be possibly charged for its possession, in accordance with the law of the land. The person found to be the main culprit who possessed the unlicensed firearm would be charged, remanded, and subsequently fined or imprisoned. I know that people have varying opinions on this issue. However, the crux of the matter is this: the law is designed to protect the citizens of the country. What happens if a child finds the weapon and accidently shoots himself or someone else? The owner must be held accountable for his/her foolish actions.

Similar to the purpose of the laws of the land, laws and principles are designed to preserve the purpose of God's kingdom. When you understand, you will discover that the heart of God is to preserve and execute His purpose for all generations. Your level of righteousness is dependent on your level of obedience to laws. We need to understand that God deeply cares about His people and that He has good intent towards them. I pray that we would have a deeper understanding and appreciation for His laws so that we can partner with God at a deeper level. If we do not buy into the philosophy of God's laws, then nothing will happen on earth, and we will live average and unproductive lifestyles. We desperately need His laws in order to survive on the earth.

Key No. 3: Apply the Laws

Applying laws is the hallmark of righteousness. A man is known for what he does, not for what he thinks. If you pay keen attention to mankind today, you will agree that the successful ones are those who apply laws and principles. If you want to maintain a healthy body, then you will have to find the corresponding principles (laws) and apply them. I often hear people say, 'Life is not fair.' My response to that is 'Life is only fair to those people who apply laws.' If you just sit and pray, you will not accomplish anything in life. A lot of believers are just sitting and praying and hoping that some miracle will fall in their paths. You need to learn to apply God's laws, which will bring about the difference in your life. This is what will transition you from a place of mediocrity to productivity.

Applying righteousness in the workplace does not include only prayer; it also includes following company policies, not engaging in gossiping, obeying leaders in authority, working diligently, loving others, being creative and innovative in your work, going the extra miles, being open to correction, disciplining, and upgrading yourself. These are some of the qualities that will give a position of influence in the workplace so that you can expand God's kingdom.

The Wealth of the Wicked is laid up for the Righteous!

In closing, I want to explain the above statement taken from the Scripture. Remember that a righteous person is one who is governed by laws and principles. Many times, believers quote this extract, and, with limited understanding, they declare it over their lives. The acquisition of wealth has laws. Also, when you get the wealth, there are some laws that you have to apply in order to maintain it. You cannot get wealth by sitting down merely in a position of prayer and expect God to drop it through your windows. You have to get up and work hard for it. If you have business ideas, you have to process those ideas and create your desired business. You also have to market your product in order for it to sell. I am not saying that I am a business expert, but I am bothered by the fact that too many believers are living in a fantasy world. Therefore, I am challenging you to go about doing your kingdom business in a righteous manner—applying God's principles in your life-and then you will see the difference that it will make in your world.

CHAPTER 14

The Shield of Faith

Now faith is being sure of what we hope for and certain of what we
do not see.

—Hebrews 11:1 (NIV)

THE ACTIVATION AND power of faith is dependent upon two
variables: 'now' and 'is'. As insignificant as they might seem, there
is tremendous power to these two words. Why? These two words actually
describe God's kingdom. The reign and rule is not something that will
happen; it's actually here. God really lives in the 'now' time zone and He
always 'is'; this is why He reveals Himself as 'I Am'. Given that He is 'I Am',
you must always respond, through faith, to God, who requires and demands
immediate response to Him.

What is Faith?

I once heard Mike Murdock describe faith simply as 'confidence in
God'. The dictionary describes faith as 'confidence or trust in a person or
thing, or belief that is not based on proof'. In what do you believe? That is
the bottom line. I like to define faith as 'the expression of one's belief'. True
faith is all about expression because if you believe something in your heart,
then your lifestyle must reflect that belief. The Bible says:

> And without faith it is impossible to please God, because anyone who
> comes to him must believe that he exists and that he rewards those who
> earnestly seek him. (Heb. 11:6; NIV)

In the context of this Scripture, the word 'please' means 'accept'.
Therefore, faith is what makes you acceptable unto the Lord. God evaluates
me as usable based on my faith. That is why based on faith only can I function
in His kingdom. God constantly tests our faith because that determines

the substance of which we are really made. Faith is the substance and the evidence! Have you ever gone to a store, restaurant, or office and noticed a sign: 'Employees Only?' The managers are essentially saying that only people who are employees have access beyond a certain boundary. You may look like an employee; you may have the same education as an employee; you may talk like an employee; however, if you are not an employee nor have been given permission, you will not gain access to the territory.

Faith works on that principle! The closer you want to get to God, the more faith you will be required to have. Why? God will tell you to do something that your mind will question, but it takes faith to do it. When God tested Abraham, there was no cheerleader around to egg him on by saying, 'You go Abraham!' He was by himself. Most of the times, faith is a lonely place, but the beauty about it is that all it requires is movement.

Believing that He Exists is Good But Not Good Enough!

Too many people base their faith solely on the fact that God exists, and they are satisfied with that. Given that God exists, what does this mean for you? It clearly means that we must fashion our lives in a way that is pleasing to God. The only way that we can accomplish this is to be faithful to His Word, regardless of what we are facing, knowing that there is great purpose attached to our trial. Let's look at what the other portion of the Scripture says, 'He is a rewarder of those who earnestly seek him' (Heb. 11:6; Amplified Bible). The key message in this declaration is that only those who seek Him diligently will be rewarded. Therefore, faith also requires a diligent spirit. What is this saying? In brief, a diligent person is a person who works hard by applying the right principles that are pertinent to the job. For example, if you were working for someone, your mentality would be to please that person by not only working hard but also by learning the ways of that person, communicating with that person, learning the dislikes of that person, being truthful and honest, etc. This is the same approach that we have to take with God. We have to see Him as our employer and must earnestly desire to seek and please Him.

The Danger of Seeking!

Whenever you seek something, you become vulnerable to that thing. For example, people who hunt for animals become vulnerable to the prey. Why?

STANLEY R. SAUNDERS

In order to catch the prey, they have to invade its territory. Likewise, when you seek God, you become exposed to His nature, His attitude, character, and love. If you seek diligently, you will capture His heart and your life will be completely changed. Consequently, I want to challenge you to get to know the ways of the Lord. There is so much more to experience! Don't think that you have arrived! Sad to say, you have not because you have not yet experienced even an ounce of God. Let's conclude our study of faith by looking at what I call 'The Faith Cycle'.

The Faith Cycle

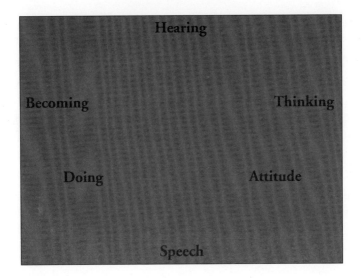

The Faith Cycle:
Hearing>thinking>attitude>saying>doing>becoming

We want to study this cycle because in it are principles that we can apply to our lives. First of all, a cycle is 'a sequence of events that are repeated again and again, especially a casual sequence' (Encarta Dictionary). In other words, a specific action leads to another action, which then produces another action, and it goes on and on. The Bible says:

> So faith comes from hearing the message. And the message that is heard is the word of Christ. (Romans 10:17; NIRV)

Hearing

It is comforting to know that the primary sense that God appeals to is our hearing, which is the gateway to faith. Therefore, one of the principles for having a great faith—life is to manage or regulate your hearing. How can you achieve this? One of the things that you have to do, is to decide what you want to hear in the midst of a negative world. Consider that we live in a time when everybody is saying that it's difficult to have financial freedom because of the global economic downturn. What do you think about this?

Your Hearing Affects Your Thinking

When you are constantly hearing something, it will definitely frame your thinking. Hence it is imperative to feed your mind with good reports. To whose report are you listening? Do yourself a favour! Create a *'hearing-thinking'* atmosphere in your house, workplace, neighbourhood, church community, or wherever you have been planted. Become connected to books, podcast, tapes, videos, CDs, friends, mentors, or anything that will positively feed your mind to where you want to go in life. Be proactive and take a stand when it comes to this area in your life. If you have to change your association in your workplace or church community, then do it because if you do not regulate your hearing, you will believe the negative reports, and they will produce barrenness in your life.

Attitude

The longer I live, the more I realize the impact of attitude on life. Attitude, to me, is more important than facts. It is more important than the past, the education, the money, than circumstances, than failure, than successes, than what other people think or say or do. It is more important than appearance, giftedness or skill. It will make or break a company . . . a church . . . a home. The remarkable thing is we have a choice everyday regarding the attitude we will embrace for that day. We cannot change our past . . . we cannot change the fact that people will act in a certain way. We cannot change the inevitable. The only thing we can do is play on the one string we have, and that is our attitude. I am convinced that life is 10 percent what happens to me and 90 percent of how I react to it. And so it is with you . . . we are in charge of our Attitudes.

–Charles R. Swindoll

Attitude is a certain feeling or disposition about a person or thing. It's important to note that thinking creates attitude. In general, your thinking determines whether your attitude is positive or negative. As a result, you cannot separate your thinking from your attitude, and the latter determines your destiny. There is a famous quote that says, 'Your attitude determines your altitude.' If you don't have a positive attitude, you will have problems in every area of your life because you will always be in conflict with people. You can tell where somebody is heading by the attitude he or she portrays. I was speaking to the manager of a prominent business to determine what the criteria for promotion on the job were. He told me that the first criterion is having a good attitude. He also mentioned that there are some people who would never be promoted because of their attitude, and they would likely lose their jobs. I agree with Charles Swindoll that we can control our attitudes. I think that people need to take control over their attitudes, and then they will have better control over their lives. If you don't take charge over your emotions, you will make some decisions that you will regret. Think about this: If you are angry with your boss, that does not change the fact that he or she is your boss. Therefore, your ill feelings towards your boss do not make the situation better. Sometimes we hold ill feelings towards God and/or people when things do not go the way we want. We need to chastise our negative emotions constantly; otherwise, we will end up between a rock and a hard place.

Speech

> You shall also decide and decree a thing, and it shall be established for you; and the light [of God's favor] shall shine upon your ways.
> –Job 22:28 (Amplified Bible)

Have you ever spoken to someone who is angry? When you are angry or bitter about a situation, you are not inclined to speak well about it. As a result, your speech will become impure. Many times, we tend to say things that we later regret. There is a famous song that says, 'It's too late to apologise.' The purpose of this 'Faith Cycle' is to help you take charge of your attitude so that your speech becomes pure at all times. Accordingly, you will not have to live apologising every day since you will be voicing better decisions. The weapon of speech is powerful because our words can actually create life in the midst of darkness.

The Scripture above says, 'Decide and decree a thing, and it shall be established for you . . . ' The key principle here is that, personally, you have to decide to speak well about a situation in spite of what you are going through, and then it shall be established. What will be established? The will of God for you or for a place will become a reality. In order for this to happen, we must each be willing to stand and say, 'I want the will of God for this community.' You may agree that there are not many people who would willingly do that nowadays. When believers are fed up, they tend to call judgement on a place or person. From my experience, nobody tends to listen to a person who constantly speaks judgement. When you speak positively about a place or person, it gives you an advantage. Why? Psychologically, you begin to see what you speak; as a result, you will be able to function in that environment with a positive outlook.

Doing and Becoming

'What you are doing is what you are practicing. What you have become is a result of what you have been practicing.'

The expression of faith is in doing. All the other stages of the cycle are preparing you to be a 'doing' person. All the great people in life are known for what they do, not for what they thought about doing. Michael Jordan was a great basketball player because of what he did? What did he do? Jordan spent hours repeatedly practising the right techniques. Consequently, he became great in his field. If you want to become a great person of faith, then you just have to do what God tells you to do, in spite of what is happening around you. If you have an idea to do something, such as improve your workplace, start your own business, or improve your family, then apply faith. Applying faith would mean to take some steps that would get you close to your goals. A lot of times we tend to think that faith is only when we reach our final destiny because we confuse 'faith' and 'fate'. This is unfortunate! I am telling you that it takes great *faith* to take steps in life. Don't be afraid of your critics! Step out and you will be surprised to see the doors that God will open for you.

STANLEY R. SAUNDERS

Final Encouragement!

If you apply the principles in this book, then you will experience tremendous breakthroughs in your life. Life is a journey, and I want you to enjoy the ride. Be in charge of your life by taking hold of your thinking. You have everything within you to achieve whatever your heart desires. Don't allow anyone or anything to shatter your self-esteem. Just walk with confidence, knowing that all things will work for your good.

Closing Prayer

'Father, I pray for the people who have read this book. I pray that You will help them to not only keep the principles in their hearts but also to live by them; also, that each will endeavour to begin or continue to be an impact in this world. I pray for Your blessings and strength as they continue to walk in truth and light. Give your people divine ideas so that they can function in their environments. I ask all this in Jesus's name. *Amen!*

REFERENCES

http://www.thelisteningprogram.com/How_TLP_Works_Ear_Brain_Connection.asp

biblegateway.com

blueletterbibile.com

Dictionary.com

Merriam-Webster Online Dictionary

thefreedictionary.com

The Names of God: Lester Sumrall

Understanding seasons of change by Myles Munroe

Understanding your Potential—Myles Munroe

wikepedia.com

INDEX

E

Ephesians
  6:10-20, 90
Exodus
  15:23-24, *98*
  17:5-6, *83*
Ezekiel
  22:30, *108*
  36:26, *39*

F

Facebook, 120
faith, 47, 80, 102, 110-11, 141-43
Faith Cycle, 143-46
fall of man, 20
farmer, 63-65, 74-75, 81. *See also*
    God; gardener
fig tree, 70-71
forgiveness, 52, 109, 134-35
freewill, 27
French Revolution, 15

G

gardener, 61, 63-66, 72, 75-76. *See*
    also God; farmer
Garden of Eden, 128
Genesis
  1:26-27, *16*
  1:26-28, *56*
  6:5, *21*
  6:9, *137*
Gethsemane, 96
God, 7, 16-50, 52-54, 56-84, 89-90,
    92-120, 122-29, 131-43, 145-
    46, 149
  armour of, 89, 91

grace of, 27, 41, 48
heart of, 24, 43, 99, 112, 139
names of, 101
See also Heavenly Father; gardener;
    farmer; silversmith
Goliath (Philistine champion), 114,
    127-28
grace, 27, 29, 41, 47-50, 53, 70, 93,
    96, 104, 110, 137

H

heart, 17-18, 40-43
  spiritual, 42
Heavenly Father, 20, 96, 99-100, 105.
    See also God
Hebrews
  4:12, *67*
  11:1, *141*
  11:6, *141*, *142*
  12:2, *80*
Herod (king of Judea), 122
Hosea
  4:6, *103*
humility, 29-30, 34, 73

I

identity, 55-60, 84
intercession, 106-9
Iraq, 15
Isaiah
  43:18-21, *82*
  46:10, *80*
  54:17, *65*
  57:17, *30*
Israel, 58, 82-83, 93, 98, 101, 118,
    128. *See also* Jacob (Hebrew
    patriarch)

seek comprehension of the laws,
139
apply the laws, 140
Romans
   5:12-14, *20*
   8:1-2, *49*
   8:26, *111*
   10:17, *143*
   13:14, *92*
   13:1-5, *72*

S

sacrificial mentality, 94
salvation, 34, 43, 54, 115, 126-28, 132
1 Samuel
   13:13-14, *93*
   15:22, *134*
   17:45-47, *128*
Samuel (Hebrew prophet), 93
Sarah (wife of Abraham), 100
Satan, 21, 32, 133. *See also* Dragon;
   Prince of Darkness; devil
Saul (king of Israel), 73, 93, 133
Saunders, Stanley R.
   Developing a Spiritual Warfare
     Mentality in the Midst of the
     Valley, 26
Silas (apostle), 108-9
silversmith, 76. *See also* God
sin (*see also* disobedience), 17, 20-22,
   29-30, 46, 48-49, 52-53, 105,
   121-22, 126, 134
slavery, 33, 51-53
sowing and reaping, law of, 27, 29
spiritual slavery, 51
spiritual warfare, 15, 17-18, 20, 22-
   26, 45, 55, 73-74, 89, 91, 95,
   112, 147
stony heart, 39-40

Sumrall, Lester
   The Names of God, 101
Swindoll, Charles, 145

T

1 Timothy
   2:1-4, *107*
Tomatis, Alfred A., 119
trust, 76-79, 81, 83, 98, 100
truth, 121-25

U

United States of America, 4, 15
Uprising (Bob Marley and the
   Wailers), 51

V

valley, 26-27
valley of bad choices, 27, 31
valley of destiny, 27, 31-32, 35, 52-54,
   57-59, 65, 69, 97, 103
Vietnam War, 15
Vine, 65-66, 68-69, 74. *See also* Word
   of God

W

warfare, 15, 112-13
warfare mentality, 16-17, 19-21, 26,
   93, 103, 147
Washington Post, 15
Word of God (*see also* Vine), 25, 32, 37,
   40, 48, 62, 66-69, 71-72, 89-90,
   93, 98-99, 102, 110, 116, 129
World War I, 15
World War II, 15
worship, 94